Hey Big Spender
'get an emotional grip'

Hey Big Spender
'get an emotional grip'

Includes RED Dot Shopping designed to reduce your weekly spending by up to a third!

Ann Carver

authorHOUSE

AuthorHouse™
1663 Liberty Drive
Bloomington, IN 47403
www.authorhouse.com
Phone: 1-800-839-8640

© 2013 by Ann Carver. All rights reserved.

No part of this book may be reproduced, stored in a retrieval system, or transmitted by any means without the written permission of the author.

Published by AuthorHouse   02/06/2013

ISBN: 978-1-4817-8287-6 (sc)
ISBN: 978-1-4817-8286-9 (hc)
ISBN: 978-1-4817-8288-3 (e)

Any people depicted in stock imagery provided by Thinkstock are models, and such images are being used for illustrative purposes only.
Certain stock imagery © Thinkstock.

This book is printed on acid-free paper.

Because of the dynamic nature of the Internet, any web addresses or links contained in this book may have changed since publication and may no longer be valid. The views expressed in this work are solely those of the author and do not necessarily reflect the views of the publisher, and the publisher hereby disclaims any responsibility for them.

Contents

1. In Debt on All Levels 1
2. Just the Tip 17
3. Get Change 27
4. RED The Spending Pirate 43
5. RED Dot Shopping 53
6. Dealing with RED 59
7. Emotional Shopping Fix 71
8. Vision & Goals 89
9. For 'Richer or Poorer' 99
10. Money Memories 107
11. Conscious Shopping 113
12. Budge *it* 123
13. Real Stories Real People 131

A BIG thank you to;

Steve my husband and my rock. Conroy Williams from Hampshire School for Social Entrepreneurs, Linda Taylor from Portsmouth CC, Guri Hummelsund from UnLtd for all believing in me and igniting the spark. Lee Yeats from Affinity Sutton Housing Association for seeing the potential in this work and enabling it to grow, Amanda Jean Baptise from Actis for the mentoring, John and Prim Sidgreaves for their support; Arun Speakers, for nurturing my voice; Lauren Easterbrook and Phil Strawn for the artwork, plus all other acquaintances and friends and many great teachers and coaches I have met and learnt from on this journey.

About the Author

In 2009 Ann was awarded a place at Hampshire School For Social Entrepreneurs to develop Hey Big Spender; she is also qualified in motivation coaching and NLP (behaviour change), and is a public speaker and member of Toastmasters International, prior to this Ann was a popular student and teacher of Iyengar yoga for 17 years.

However for over a decade Ann went on an emotional spending spree, she became addicted to retail therapy after a family tragedy struck. Little did she know that shopping to express her emotions would spiral so out of control. Ann's mortgage climbed from £10,000 to £100,000 and she racked up over £27,000 in unsecured debt. A few other facts that added to her debts were;

1. Growing up a working-class girl she knew how to earn and spend money, but not how to manage it
2. Being self-employed with limited business skills
3. Undervaluing her life after going through abuse

Ann states that her financial mess reflected her emotional and mental battle with life. Conventional help such as remortgaging, loans and financial advice simply fuelled Ann's addiction, as it enabled her to access money and disguise her problems. Ann's wake-up call came after she almost lost the family home. Desperate to change she searched for ways to change her habits and behaviours. She learnt from experts such as Tony Robbins, Keith Tondeur and John Cummuta. And she took time to face her

Ann Carver

demons. This approach enabled her to pay her debts back in record time and to become free of past guilt and shame.

As Ann reached solid ground, the credit crunch hit. Ann has made it her business and mission to show people how to rein their spending habits in and live more fulfilling lives.

Intro

Hi and a *BIG* warm welcome!

Has shopping lost its sparkle but at the same time you feel addicted to it? Maybe you see life through a poverty mind-set, so no matter how much you have it's never quite enough? Or are you in the habit of fooling people that your spendthrift lifestyle is affordable, yet deep down you're struggling to keep a lid on it? You know it's only a matter of time before the truth comes out.

What are your spending habits costing you?

Your emotional and impulse spending habits are probably costing you a lot more money and anxiety than you actually realise or ever bargained for. Perhaps debt's already weighing heavily on your mind or maybe the pleasure of retail therapy has turned into nightmare? And although it's costing you your smile and your quality of life big time, another part of you just can't seem to stop.

Do you class yourself as?

- A spendaholic or a shopping addict?
- Overwhelmed with too much month and not enough money?
- Stinking rich, unfulfilled and shopping for the sake of it?

Emotional spending destroys relationships, causes overwhelming stress and anxiety shows its ugly face on a daily basis.

Once in debt, you dread the phone ringing, as it's more than likely creditors making demanding and pressurizing calls. And the postman has swapped delivering exciting parcels in exchange for heavy demands. You may have truly believed that the items you bought genuinely made you feel better, and they probably did until the addiction kicked in. But now the long-term price tag has attached itself to the quick-fix feel-good factor. The designer bags feel more like heavy bricks. And all along, you were harmlessly shopping for confidence, happiness, and love, but instead you are now experiencing, unhappiness, worry, debt or depression, which was never part of the deal. Ironically these consequences are what you were spending money to originally escape from!

- If you think that spending money is the answer to your problems then how come they have got worse instead of better?

Why this book?

The intentions of this book is for you to recognise and get to grips with your out-of-control, sometimes crazy emotional spending habits that trigger you to spend, spend, spend, time and time again. The aim of *Hey Big Spender* is to enable you to love your money and life beyond the shop shelves—not *instead of* but *more than*. Different people have different needs. For some people, opening their eyes to the amount of money that impulse and emotional spending is costing them is all they need to execute change. Other people have deeper-rooted emotions that need to be recognised and addressed in order to defuse their spending triggers.

- Are you ready to get a grip?
- Or do you want to continue to let more and more of your money and life slip from your wallet / purse into the till?

Hey Big Spender Guarantee

If you don't love your money, then someone else definitely will. Bank managers love your money, as do loan companies and every shop imaginable, not to mention the people in your life with whom you over generously share it. Getting to grips with your emotional spending habits and behaviours that affect your relationship with money is the golden key to success, I guarantee.

*Financial success is the ability to learn
from expensive mistakes.*

Who's in control?

- Do you often buy items and later *(perhaps even the same day)* wonder what the hell you were thinking?
- Perhaps you hate the weekly grind of food shopping and want to get it over with as quickly as possible, but spend a small fortune in the process?
- Maybe spending money has become a process, like driving a car, and you give very little thought to what you are buying or what it's costing you?

Know that all scenarios are costing you big time as you're costly spending habits have now weaved themselves into your weekly or even daily life patterns so cleverly that you find it hard to distinguish between your wants and needs.

I guarantee that if you're not in control of your emotions *(whether happy or sad)* whilst shopping, you will easily overspend money, regardless of whether or not you can afford to. Whether it's your own desires or powerful external influences driving you to buy, such as attractive advertising campaigns *(especially sexy ones)* that somehow seduce you to part with your cash, know that both internal and external pulls on your wallet / purse strings can only be controlled and changed by one person: and that's you.

Ann Carver

Yes consumerism is like a giant magnet drawing you in, but it's a two-way street. You and I have to learn to develop our *no* muscles and walk on by temptation before it strikes.

It's the same as when you're in the driver's seat of your car; only you can change gear and steer the wheel. You will never be able to stop the temptations that are constantly in your path, but you can change how you react to them. Likewise, you cannot change the layout of the road ahead, but you can change the direction or find the best route through. Yes, you are the change. And to get change with your spending habits, you must take control and learn to nurture your relationship with money for the better of your wealth (incidentally, wealth stems from the term well-being).

> *Don't wish it were easier;*
> *wish you were better.*
> —Jim Rohn

Result

Because you have picked up this book, you can be assured that your journey of breaking free from emotional and impulse spending trap has started. I want you to know that freedom from this is achievable, no matter how dependent you feel on shopping and spending money right now. Believe me when I say that there is a way out for anyone who wants to find the exit, and learning to harness the emotions that create your spending habits and behaviours is the golden key to finding it. There is no doubt that you will reap deep and meaningful rewards from learning about how you and your money tick; instead of getting poorer, you'll become enriched. Yes, you have to put the work in, but believe me, it will pay off and return to you priceless results that are worth all your efforts.

It's now time to take your designer shades off, my friend, so that one day soon you will discover the real inner riches and treasures of life from the inside out, *not* the outside in. Why? So you can have money and happiness and re-design your destiny.

Tools of the Trade

Listed below is a short description of some of the tools you will be using in more detail as you work through this book. You already hold most of the tools in your power, it's just a matter of tapping into them, and others can be learnt and mastered with the help of this book. The best thing of all is that they don't cost a dime and they are already in your possession, like treasure waiting to be found on the inside.

Body Language - Learn to use your body language to the best of your advantage, 55% of how you communicate is reflected through your body, it's the first thing the shop assistant sees! They can see if you are shopping with your eyes shut and are easy prey or not.

Mental Focus - Concentrate your focus on what you want, not what you don't like getting from the beginning to the end of the day in pocket!

Power Questions - The power is in the asking. Ask;

- *What do I intend to spend today?*
- *What do I need learn about money?*
- *How can I become financially free?*

Questions are like matches that strike an inner light, your brain will always answer them.

Power Words - Good words are the equivalent of good soul food, great words are even greater! Speak wealthy words over your money such as: *'I am behaving and saving an absolute fortune today.'*

Behaviour Change Techniques (NLP) - Enable YOU to change. Red Dot Shopping will change your shopping habits for good. Unless you change there will be NO change.

Metaphors - Are powerful visual aids to empower learning. Look out for RED the Spending Pirate later in this book. Once you recognise his antics you can easily outsmart him.

Vision and Goals - Look to the future and make it happen, step by step.

Boundaries - Keep you and your money safe. Put healthy spending boundaries in place.

Education - Learning about money and life should be interesting and enjoyable, then it inspires you to want to carry on growing to the best of your ability.

Hey Big Spender 'get an emotional grip'

> *The more you know, the more luck you have.*
> —Chinese saying

A Crucial Message

I want this book to teach you a lot, but there's one main thing I want you to grasp, as without it you *will not* change, you *will not* grow, and that would be a BIG shame. In fact, it's almost guaranteed that you'll stay exactly as you are. This one most important thing is that you *must* <u>take action</u>. (If you choose not to, please learn to accept and love your life just as it is.)

Why should you get to grips?

As you begin to change the way you spend money and conduct your life, people's heads will turn, as they'll notice that you're wearing a new radiant look from the inside out. This wins easily over having any designer brand or expensive outfit, as you become the real deal. Overspending and debt put massive pressure on your personal and professional life. You create a false image, and before long, you find yourself struggling to keep up with the expectations that yourself and others have of you. It's easy to fall into the trap of focusing on what you think you should look like and miss out on true happiness. When you do begin to change, you suddenly realise that you much prefer the person you've become.

Personally and Professionally

Personally I am not a financial advisor or a money expert, but I am woman who messed up with money because I simply got addicted to spending it. But right now I feel very fortunate in this credit crunch to have no huge debts and no nasty letters flying through the door. I can answer my phone with ease and arrive at the checkout without worrying whether I'll have enough money to pay. I feel happier, more confident, and more optimistic that I have ever felt. I am living life with passion and purpose to help others change too. However, rest assured that life for me wasn't always this rosy, as back in 2005, my money and life reflected a nightmare that I had created from my reckless emotional spending habits.

I came to my senses and began to realise that while conventional methods, such as getting financial advice and borrowing to pay my debts back, might help, they do nothing to help me address the underlying emotions that trigger me to spend. They only address the debt, which was not the problem—I was! Thankfully, I kept determinedly digging until I eventually found solutions that put me on the right path. After I got my debts under control, I then decided to take an alternative approach to help me get my head around my poor mindset and behaviour towards money and life.

I trained and qualified as a life coach and in NLP (neuro linguistic programming, or behaviour change), as I knew that I needed to set goals and move me and my mindset on. Taking this approach enabled me to climb out of debt in record time and come out the other side more emotionally sound and a better money and life manager. As the credit crunch hit, a desire ignited to help other people in similar situations get a grip. In 2009, I was awarded a place at Hampshire School for Social Entrepreneurs (www.hsse.org.uk). In plain English, social entrepreneurs are people who see or experience problems either in their personal lives, within their families, in their communities, or in society—and then make it their mission to do something about it. I thought I had no chance of a place because I had messed up, but they said I was the perfect candidate. After my own personal debt experience I soon learnt that there is very little help in the UK to help people learn better habits and behaviours around money, as our consumerist society is geared up for us to spend money not to manage it.

The *Hey Big Spender* concept is proving to build people's confidence and better their money management skills, especially in tempting day-to-day situations, but most of all, they are valuing themselves as human beings more than materialism—not *instead of* but *more than*, as realistically we live in a consumerist society, so balance is absolute key. It's awesome to see this work making a difference in other people's lives. The most successful strategy that I have developed is RED Dot Shopping, which helps you to resist temptation whilst out shopping, online, or anywhere else you're inclined to spend what you don't intend. This evolved out of my own need to discipline my spending and keep my money safe, and the more I put it into practice, the savvier I became. I have now mastered the art of *'behaving and saving'* myself from the depths of debt and despair (as well as a small fortune!). But mostly I gained a sense of security and valued my money and life with newfound appreciation. To me, this felt more priceless than any of material possessions I ever bought. It feels empowering to outsmart the big guys and be one step ahead of the clever marketing techniques.

> *'I've never been able to save for the future, and I feel I have always wasted money on things. When I felt unhappy, I impulse spent to take my mind off my problems, but I always felt worse afterwards. Because of Hey Big Spender, I now have the knowledge to change my life for the better. I have grown in confidence and now know why I spent in the way I did'.*
>
> —Aimy C

Seduced by Consumerism

Consumerism purposely seduces you into buying as many items, as often as it can. Before I got to grips with my own emotional spending habits, I was forever allowing myself to be seduced by consumerism, and I was paying for it big time too! I said yes too often and too easily, instead of *no, no, no!* I also allowed other people—family, friends, and peers in my career—to control me too. I'd become a people pleaser.

Yet personally, I always wanted so much more . . . more happiness, more fulfilment, more exhilarating moments, more purpose to life, more for my family, more love and unity from my parents, and more attention from my brothers. I also wanted more material things, such as a house by the sea, a horse for my youngest daughter and a flat for my eldest, and for my husband to be able to retire at an earlier age than sixty-five. But all my spending habits did was lead me further away from my dreams.

Dependable solutions to my debt, such as financial advice, didn't recognise the fact that I had a spending problem. Loans and credit simply fuelled my addiction and piled my debts higher, and that any budgeting I managed to do would be ignored or forgotten about when the urge to *'spend and mend Ann'* kicked in. However, when I began to feel the pain and consequences of my behaviour, I finally woke up and took responsibility. Why do we humans wait until we are practically on our knees before we decide to get our act together? As a result, I now feel truly fulfilled and have my freedom and confidence back. One key thing I have learnt from my emotional shopping experience is this: *We own our lives, and we can choose to make them priceless gifts.*

> *We are all standing in our own acre of diamonds.*
> —Earl Nightingale

Coming Out

I feel as though wearing our hearts on our sleeves about our money crisis is the new *coming out*. Up until now us Brits have been more open about our sexuality than we have our money. I've reached a stage in my life where I feel unafraid to speak openly about my debt situation, as I much prefer being open and honest and unashamed. The moment I held my hands up about my spending problem was the moment my journey to true debt freedom began. It's become like a real-life game of *tap and pass it on*, as this work continues to impact and change other people's lives. The more real

I am with myself, the more I relate to other people in an authentic manor, which enables them to open up about their own situations. Then we can relate to each other as human beings, not humans pretending it's all right when it isn't!

My story made local headlines in the *Portsmouth News* in 2010, and I was then asked to tell my story on *This Morning TV*. After that, people would approach me in the street and in the supermarket and tell me their stories (which was an absolute honour by the way), and the conversation would often end with a hug to a complete stranger! In fact, this heartfelt response has encouraged me to continue with this journey. I am sad to say that certain family members truly thought I was a disgrace, but this problem is hardly recognised compared other to addictions such as alcohol and drugs in the UK. I hope that one day they can see the bigger picture with more understanding. I am not writing this out of spite but out of fact. So although I'm not a financial advisor or a money genius, I am a person who got caught up in the net of debt through my careless spending habits and overpowering emotions, but thankfully I got desperate enough to want find a way out.

Financial knots can be untangled, and once undone, they'll shed pounds of worry!

1

In Debt on All Levels

Debt affected my money, my mind, my emotions, my body, my health, my relationships, my career, my home, my soul, my future, and my entire world.
—Ann Carver

Emotional Debt

I owed it to myself to feel better. Each shopping trip meant I got to try on new feelings and brighter things (to cover up the darkness that was going on internally), plus I got to put the precious feelings in a bag and take them home. However, when I arrived home, it was as if the material possessions became empty shells, as the feelings I'd bought into at the time of the purchase quickly disappeared. Often I had no idea why I'd bought what I did.

The seed of my spending addiction was planted when I was walking through Havant town with my head held low. It should have been a happy day as it was my birthday, but it was traumatically sad as my mother had died suddenly, precisely a year before, her funeral fell on my birthday too, which was a double whammy.

Suddenly, a bright red daisy jumper that was displayed on the manikin in the shop window distracted me from my glum state; it was as if an instant uplift had been infused. The next thing I knew, I was in the dressing room of the shop, glancing at myself in the mirror. A smile widened my face. 'Happy birthday Ann', I said to my reflection. Not wanting to take the happier feelings off, I paid for the jumper and continued my walk through the town. I was now feeling different, somewhat optimistic compared to my previous mood. As I walked, I began to notice that people were smiling at me and I was smiling back. As time went by, I would hear a voice inside of me say:

> *Let's go shopping.*
> *Go on, you deserve it.*
> *Oh, to hell with the cost.*
> *You work hard enough.*
> *You're not doing any harm*

This seemingly healing way to help *mend Ann*, to reach out to the shop shelves to express and soothe my emotions, became my new obsession. At first, it was controlled and purely used to escape the dark clouds that loomed over my personality approximately two months before the anniversary of my mother's death. But then life dealt yet another double tragedy, as my eldest brother, David, died of a brain tumour within six months of being diagnosed. Then my father passed away too. This fuelled my urge to shop, and it distracted me from overwhelming feelings that were extremely tough to face. And so my shopping habit spiralled out of control.

Shopping Moods

As my shopping habit took hold, any mood would do, happy or sad, lonely or depressed, with or without the kids. I'd use any excuse to jump in the car and take flight to the shops. I also began to shop straight after work. At the time I was a dynamic yoga teacher, a mother, and a wife. I would do the best possible job I could in these responsible roles, which also kept me occupied, but as soon as it was time to wind down and put my feet up, I would hear a voice inside me say, *You've made everyone else feel better; now it's your turn.* I needed no convincing.

A typical shopping spree would start with lunch, and then I would browse. Sometimes I would spend a little; other times a lot. Sometimes I would shop locally in Havant; when I needed more of buzz, I would head off for Gun Wharf Quays wonderland of shops.

Shopping becoming an addiction

Little did I know that retail therapy would become a full-blown addiction? All I knew was that shopping distracted me for a while and made me smile. However, as the years went by, debt became my new harsh reality. As well as the huge financial burden, I also hid the truth (and the bags) from my husband! Once again, I began to suffer overwhelming worry and anxiety, but this time it stemmed from the financial debt I had created, which at times seemed worse than the deaths. I dreaded the phone ringing, as most of the calls were from creditors demanding money. As soon I heard the postman, I would race to the front door so other family members wouldn't beat me to it. The brown envelopes filled me with heaviness upon opening them, and as I glanced at the outstanding figures, my stomach would be in knots. And month by month, the figures increased. On many occasions, I arrived at the checkout to pay for the weekly shopping, only to hear that my method of payment had been declined. And so my world began to collapse.

Retail therapy is a harmless act isn't it?

So originally emotional spending started as what I thought was a harmless act that allowed me to feel better within myself. The era of easy credit combined with a new trend of superstores opening their wide doors on the outskirts of Portsmouth, where I live, also helped me to blow my spending habits and debts out of proportion. The initial buzz of consumer wonderland meant that I could have anything I wanted. I remember the thrill and excitement of the journey to the shops and the anticipation and surprise element once I arrived. So instead of using retail therapy on a small scale, I used it on a big one.

Once in recovery, it took me a long time to find solutions that would not only help me change my emotional spending habits and life for the better but also sustain them and enjoy learning the process of growing in confidence and control. In the UK, financial aid to educate people about common-sense spending, especially emotional money management, is very limited (hence the reason for writing this book).

> Shopaholic Brits amass £24bn debt during downturn
> Four million women and three million men defying downturn and continuing to spend heavily, says comparison website uSwitch.
>
> The Guardian Aug 2010

When I read the above quote in the *Guardian* newspaper, I called the journalist and shared my story. As a result, the following article was published on 23 September 2010:

Confessions of a Spendaholic—and how I turned my life around

After years of spending my way through grief, my wake-up call came when I nearly lost the house—that's when things changed. Until very recently, I was what I would term a spendaholic. Growing up a working-class girl, I knew how to earn and how to spend, but not how to manage money or my emotions around it. My spending tipped from normal spending to spendaholism when I lost my mother, father, and brother in quick succession. My mother's funeral happened on my 28th birthday, and I took to shopping as my outlet to express; I couldn't stand being home alone with my sad thoughts. Over a decade I spent my way to over £27,000 of unsecured debt and the mortgage climbed from £10,000 to £100,000.

The UK as a nation suppresses its emotions, especially when it comes to talking about money troubles and death. Us Brits seem to be good at playing the game of 'let's pretend it's all right when it's not'. When you are feeling down, your friends don't know what to say, or how to treat you. But when I was out shopping, even people who didn't know me were friendly. Supposed help such as loans and financial advice to remortgage simply enabled me to pile on the pounds: they gave me the green light to spend. Trying to budget was useless while I was emotionally overwhelmed. There was no logic to my thinking and the urge to fix and spend won every time. I tried harder to be a success in my job to cover the cost of my spending, but deep down I knew I wouldn't be able to keep this up forever. My big wake-up call came when I almost lost the family house, which was now mortgaged up to the hilt. The bank manger shook her head, the credit cards declined, and this quick fix to feel good now revealed a very dark, long-term consequence. Then I got mad at myself; I now wanted to change . . . to get my head around this awful mess. Most of all I wanted to keep our house. Finally I took responsibility. On the road to my recovery, I began to write about my experience and the tools that helped along the way. I went back to full-time work in sales, read many books, and attended every motivation and money seminar going. I sold half the garden just before the recession to pay off all the unsecured debts (but not the mortgage), and I have stayed debt-free ever since. I also trained as a life coach and a public speaker to learn to set goals and find my voice. Since the credit crunch, all I have seen are others suffering around me, which has made me want to help other spendaholics and people with destructive spending habits. Spending to feel better makes your problems worse when it spirals out of control.

Ann Carver

Challenging Thought

> *I'm from the financial world, and we don't want the likes of you around, as we need people to be financially dependable, not responsible.*

A man in Brighton spoke these exact words. I'd just finished giving a talk about *Hey Big Spenders'* purpose and cause. I almost felt intimidated, but instead I stood tall, listened, and smiled, as I realised this was a sure sign that I was making a stir!

The nation is suffering the financial consequences of living in a consumerist society along with using shopping to disperse intense emotions from excitement through to sadness. A big part of me wanted to ignore this instinctive message to help others, but each time I ignored it, I got a universal nudge to carry on. Maybe spending money has been purposely designed to be easy and managing it more difficult on purpose—and as a result, we depend on other people to manage our money for us? Or maybe this guy in Brighton was exaggerating and money education is a genuine missing piece of the puzzle within society?

Notice

> *Mortgage climbed from £10,000 to £100,000; unsecured debts at £27,000.*

If I'd seen these figures on a notice board relating to my future, would it have stopped me in my tracks? Would it have made me think a bit deeper about what I was doing? To be honest, at the time, I probably wouldn't have even seen the sign or recognised that the name on it was mine. Although I can recognise and write about this now, at the time I was just doing what many other people did.

Shopping Fix

Shopping meant I could wear a smile and arrive home feeling that I'd survived yet another day. I believed it could only get better. Plus I could go out into the big wide world and enjoy being around people, having light-hearted conversation (I love people; I grew up on an estate of post-war Londoners). Plus the people I would meet whilst out shopping, like the shopkeepers and other friendly folk, wouldn't have a clue as to who I was or what I was going through. This suited me fine and enabled me to avoid any more of the tears and isolation that I felt when I was at home alone. For these reasons, retail therapy served me well, as it released the intense emotional pressure. Experiencing my life getting worse when it should have been getting better, seemed to be a pattern of mine. I was truly afraid that if I stopped to face the dark clouds, I would crack up in the face of it all—and bugger that!

Help

I did seek professional help. My first port of call was bereavement counselling, but when the woman discovered that I was a yoga teacher, she asked me if I would volunteer to help others, but I truly needed to help myself at that time. I then took myself off to the doctor. I wanted to be prescribed homeopathy, as I was breastfeeding my daughter and teaching, so the last thing I wanted was to be hooked on pharmaceutical medication. He informed me that I wasn't in the catchment area to receive homeopathy. If I'd lived five miles away, I would have been eligible. He offered me antidepressants, which I declined; they scared the hell out of me.

As a child, I had seen the damning effect that medication had had on my parents, which was one of the reasons I decided to take up yoga for my own peace of mind and future health. I made a conscious decision that day to find my own way through the tough times ahead.

I found that bereavement carries a stigma. Certain friends stopped speaking to me, as they didn't know what to say, and even a few family members pushed me away. I'm convinced that this boils down to the UK being a somewhat suppressed society. In times of real emotional need, we are conditioned to keep a stiff upper lip—or to have a stiff drink and keep on a brave face. My only remaining brother emigrated to Australia just as my older brother became ill. I became angry for quite some time, which also frightened the hell out of me. My husband was a rock through it all, although he never really understood the pain I was going through and couldn't be there 24/7.

Alternative Solutions

Initially I started spending money on alternative help, such as private counselling, homeopathy, and nutrition as I knew I couldn't depend on the NHS to grant me the help I wanted. To me, I needed this self-investment to get better. But in my search to mend Ann, I had no insight that my spending would one day make my life worse than it already was. If only I knew that no amount of shopping was ever going to be enough to fill the big empty feeling inside, the main type of support I needed was patience, love and understanding, but the loved ones I normally turned to for this were now gone and so I thought I could capture this back through alternative remedies and shopping. And it would take many years and a lot of money spent before I would realise that it was only I that could ever achieve this.

You would have thought that being a yoga teacher and student with one of the finest schools in the world would have been the perfect antidote on its own, but I have since learnt that no one is God and everyone is human. In addition, yoga was no longer my therapy, as it was in my younger years, for now it was my profession. I'd originally taken up yoga in my early twenties to overcome anxiety and depression from a rocky childhood; over the years, it strengthened my will and confidence and made me grasp a sense of appreciation for life. I never thought I would end up teaching it, but when something does you good, you can't help but pass it on.

Distraction

Yes, shopping did distract me for a while and make me smile, but it was just a temporary solution. I truly did fool myself into thinking that I could cover up my emotional hurts by disguising them in the material world. New clothes were like shields. Each time I covered up with a new jumper or headed out to lunch, I was able to shy away from the real me. I was forever promising this part of myself that I would face the hurt at another more convenient time and day—but not just now. Gradually, layer upon layer, I managed to create a disguise. Yes talking to alternative practitioners and taking remedies helped, but perhaps too subtly and slowly for my liking as I wanted mending now, I wanted the pain to go away. And shopping seemed to transform my low mood to an instant high.

At the time, this seemed a better option for me and everyone else who was directly involved, such as family and friends. I couldn't handle my personal life, and they couldn't handle me. So I began to wear a brave outlook whilst burying my true self under a big pile of stuff—much of it trash, of course.

Items Bought

If you asked me what I bought, I could barely remember 20% of it! In the beginning, it was affordable items such as clothes, ornaments for the home, and small gifts for the kids. But as the shopping bug bit, the desire to buy bigger and better items grew. Designer labels weren't important to me, for I liked to wear clothes that I felt comfortable in. However, I loved buying books, mainly self-help ones with titles that described my feelings at the time, although I rarely read them from beginning to end. I also spent lots of time and money going to yoga conventions and buying the latest fitness equipment. I even produced my own yoga video called

'Yoga Class'. I also remember buying top of the range drum kit, a BMX bike and roller blades for my daughter. As for me, I had three cars over the ten-year period and a brand new W650 Kawasaki motorbike as well as all the leathers—now that was really insane! I also spent lots of money dining out and having lunch as often as I could.

What was I thinking?

My initial emotional pulls on my purse were to transform my sad feelings. I also used to visit the shops to be around people; buying for the kids was to compensate for the family loss and to prove to them that I cared. As for the motorbike, having the freedom as a woman to explore and act out of spontaneity had always appealed to me. I learnt to ride a motorbike in my younger years to follow in the footsteps of my elder brothers. So part of me was attempting to recapture the good times. I enjoyed the ride and the open country roads for a while, but that buzz began to fade fast too as unlike in my younger years I was now riding alone. Plus I began to feel selfish as each time I went out on the motorcycle I did so without the kids.

Over the years, being in a shop was my refuge, a place where I could spend money and time in the company of people who didn't know me personally, a place where I could have light-hearted conversation and feel better for it too, but now I was taking it to the extreme.

Ultimate Truth

I began to discover that every road and shop I explored simply led further away from the direction that I needed to turn. Wasting money and time was my way of purposely distracting me from the truth. Anything to avoid letting my inner self out ... After all, *now* was not the time or the place. The buzz of shopping compared to looking at what seemed like a big black hole in my soul won easily for over a decade. Debt and extreme stress were the price tags that came with this spendthrift lifestyle. Money ran dry, the credit cards were declined, and I often had no money left to pay for essentials like household bills and food. My world began to crash. And it all started as a way to feel better about myself! Looking back now, I realise that I simply made matters ten time worse, as all retail therapy had done was fix me for a short time, and the more I bought into it, the more demanding and competitive it became. In the end, I was financially, emotionally, mentally, and spiritually broke . . . but maybe this was where I needed to get.

> *Blessed are the cracked, for they let in the light.*
> —Groucho Marx

Other Expensive Mistakes

Being self-employed with no real business knowledge was a big mistake. I call this 'having a trading without knowing how to trade'. I spent years building up my yoga classes, and I believed passionately about the benefits of it. I earned a popular reputation and was a much-loved teacher, but this was no way near enough. I learnt the basic business skills as I went along and had good people skills, but looking back now, not learning how to run a proper business had devastating consequences.

If I'd learnt business skills from the beginning, the outcome would have been different. The yoga school's non-existent philosophy in relation to running a business was purposely not taught. Students were encouraged to believe that it was wrong to focus on the money side. In fact, one particular teacher made a successful business for herself and was cut off from the school because of it. Secretly, I always admired her. When debt became a burden, I had to cease this much-loved work. I could no longer concentrate with the financial stress, plus I knew it was time to stop reshaping others and start reshaping my financial situation. This was a tough decision to make, as many of my students had been attending my classes for over eight years and meant a lot to me, but I knew it was time to let go. After all the word yoga means union in every aspect of life, to be at one physically, mentally, emotionally and financially.

I learnt a lot from this lesson. I now know that setting a vision and financially planning, for business and my personal life, is crucial. If I don't take time out to create the big picture, my dream could easily become a nightmare. And if I ever did decide to go on *Dragons' Den*, I would make sure I knew the finances inside out; otherwise, it would be the equivalent of feeding myself to them!

Family Effects

Worse of all, I was passing my spending habits down to my kids, especially my eldest daughter who had been in the eye of the storm with me. I began to see that showering my kids with gifts (often to make up for always being at work) was teaching them to expect. This lesson was the hardest to learn as I had to accept that I had messed up their lives as well as mine. As most of the time I was out working all hours to pay for all the shopping sprees at time when my older daughter especially needed my love and attention, and I am deeply sorry for that. I would also hide bags and bank statements from my husband, and I was good at pretending all was OK when I knew damn well it wasn't.

Self-Debt

The financial debt that I'd accumulated was a sure sign that I hadn't been enlightened yet. Yes, I was in debt to the creditors, but deeper than that, I was in debt to myself. I knew I owed it to myself to learn to love me just as I was and to stop escaping to the shops every time my feelings were difficult to face. And that's exactly what I did. I have also learnt that the good we do to ourselves is never wasted, as yoga did strengthen me for when I was ready to face the real world.

I truly thought I could put on a brave face and escape my turbulent feelings, but all they did was pile up inside and wait further down the road of life for another time and place. Because of ignoring them, pressure continued to build. However, when I did get brave enough to face my feelings, I soon realised that without pressure, diamonds can never be made! What I'm trying to say is that it is never too late to find the real gems in you by accepting and loving yourself just as you are, even if it means going right back to the drawing board.

My Compost of Life

My big debt resembled a heap of compost (or a big pile of crap) that was either thrown my way or that I'd self-created at various times of my life. I often wallowed in it like a hippo, but thankfully, there came a time when I learnt to sow new seeds and grow from it all. And the main thing I have learnt from life is to learn to grow in ways that create blessings out of the mess rather than make matters worse. And for this reason, I had to stop pressing the internal wealth destruct button that I was a master at working. Going through intense life crisis knocked my confidence and self worth, so I reached a stage in my life where I felt unworthy of a decent life. Whenever I received compliments or money I would bat them off or push them away.

One big thing I wanted to be free from as an adult was the guilt and shame that I'd carried around with me since my teenage years, as a result of abuse. This was the main reason that I turned to yoga many years before, and all was going fine until the triple tragedy hit. But now I wanted to drop the heavy internal baggage for good. On my journey of debt freedom, I plucked up the courage to face the part of myself that had been buried deep inside me for many years. I'd tried on numerous occasions to face my past through counselling, but I always found myself holding back the truth of my situation and convincing myself that the past is in the past, and that it where it should stay . . . until I was introduced to the Life Centre.

Letting Go

The Life Centre specifically counsels men and women who have been abused or raped. The centre was located in the heart of Chichester city, meaning that I had to walk through the shopping precinct to reach it. After the first session, I found myself anxiously running for refuge in the shops, and this made me realise how much I used shopping as a crutch. After the second session, I noticed that I walked halfway through the town before turning to the shops. However, after the third counselling session, I knew I was showing a glimpse of change, as that day I walked straight past the shops. I was just about to turn towards the car park when I saw the cathedral. I turned and headed towards it and sat in absolute peace for quite some time. Suddenly, I was overwhelmed with tears; I sobbed like a child. But the next day I felt as though a cloud had passed and the sun was beginning to shine through. I knew my outlook towards shopping and life was changing for the better, as I was dealing with the underlying feelings that had triggered me to undervalue my life for many, many years.

Blessing in Disguise

Little did I know that my mountain of debt was really my blessing in disguise, as it was the point of no return. I could no longer escape the nasty letters or the demanding phone calls or the lack of food in the cupboards. And what really hurt was when I had to say no to the kids. Yet this was another blessing because I knew it was time to start giving them more attention in proper ways, such as spending time with them and listening to them, as they were on this journey with me too. Before this wake-up call, I thought I could cover up the kids' real needs with gifts. I was hugely mistaken. This journey has taught me a lot. The blessing was that I made a conscious decision to change—to really change this time, for the better and for good. Finally, I took ownership of my life and honoured my feelings. And I decided that it was time to let go of my emotional baggage and forgive myself for how I had reacted to the past. And that's exactly what I did.

I was on my road to recovery from being a woman who didn't manage money or my personal life very well. I was changing me. I knew that I had to learn new skills, for my behaviour had been geared up to spend money as fast as I earned it. Plus, the chance of becoming financially free and living amongst the consumerist society would be slim if I didn't smarten up my act. It felt as if I'd begun to play a game of real-life monopoly, only this time I was aiming to win and play the game to my advantage.

- Why did I want to play?

Because it was time to start lining my own pocket instead of everyone else's, and I wanted to change the destiny for my children and husband, for my destructive spending had affected them *BIG* time too.

Universal Laws

As I searched and found answers, I began to learn that many of the strategies I was adopting were universal laws that had practically been around since time began. The face of debt freedom seemed a complicated task. Yet the more I looked, the more I excited I became, as I knew I was now capable of achieving what I'd set out to do. Managing my money and life, and especially my emotions, was not rocket science, but up until now, it had looked more complicated than it actually was.

On my journey to debt freedom, I had to face up to three facts:

1. I had to admit that it was *me* who created my bad spending habits and debt. That meant I had to *stop* acting recklessly, *stop* passing blame, *stop* pushing money away and *start* treating it right.
2. I also had to *stop* turning to conventional methods of help such as credit and loans and bad financial advice. These methods were the equivalent of being prescribed the wrong drugs, and as a result, my spending got worse, *not* better.

3. If I wanted to be debt-free, I had to commit to change. And that was the golden key: *I wanted to change.* I wanted to find a way out of this bloody BIG mess; I yearned for my life and money to be truly at one.

Firing Up

Thankfully, my financial mess made me angry enough to want to get on top of my problem; that spark ignited change. Anger, one of the powerful emotions I had used shopping to avoid, was shifting me out of my long period of depression. In relation to a classic British motorbike, you can't ride one without a good strong kick-start. But the biggest lesson this journey taught me, was knowing what my true values were, and number one on my list, which I realised I treasured the most, was happiness, *not* shopping! Halleluiah!

2

Just the Tip

Debt's just the tip of the iceberg for anyone with a spending problem. Debt doesn't appear out of nowhere but builds beneath the surface of a person's life for many years.

An iceberg represents the unaddressed and unseen problems that sit beneath the surface of your life. Not knowing how to deal with your problems constructively, or where to get the right help in ways that deliver the best solutions can freeze you with fear, hold you in debt to the situation and stop you moving on. However once you do learn to recognise and deal with your problems you will soon enable the iceberg to melt and feel like the salmon swimming upstream.

The word debt means to owe, so regardless if you owe any money or not, you do owe it to yourself to recognise and get to grips with the problems that have caused your habits to build and result in an iceberg effect. Spending problems build fear of the future—of what may or may not happen.

FEAR = False Evidence Appearing Real

The massive iceberg that the *Titanic* hit started life as a single snowflake. Likewise, a mass of debt can stem from one small problem, which is left to escalate out of control, by being unrecognised or simply ignored. The *Titanic* sank and many lives were lost because of a problem that was reported and ignored as the shareholders of the ship wanted to get to New York in record time.

I you are in financial debt know it's *not* the root of the problem; the unaddressed issues that built your debt and the way you have mis-managed money and life are. If you solely focus on paying your debts back and fail to recognise and address the destructive patterns of behaviour that originally built your debt, then problems that created it simply continue to grow, and later on down the road of life, guarantee your debt will once again pile high and you will be left to face it all again. I remember my mother saying '*careful you may stay like that*'. Loans pile on top of each other; people remortgage up to the hilt or worse: fall into the trap of taking out high-interest loans which can take them a lifetime to pay back. As debt grips people's lives, it overwhelms day-to-day life with extreme distress and worry.

It's not the money but the manager

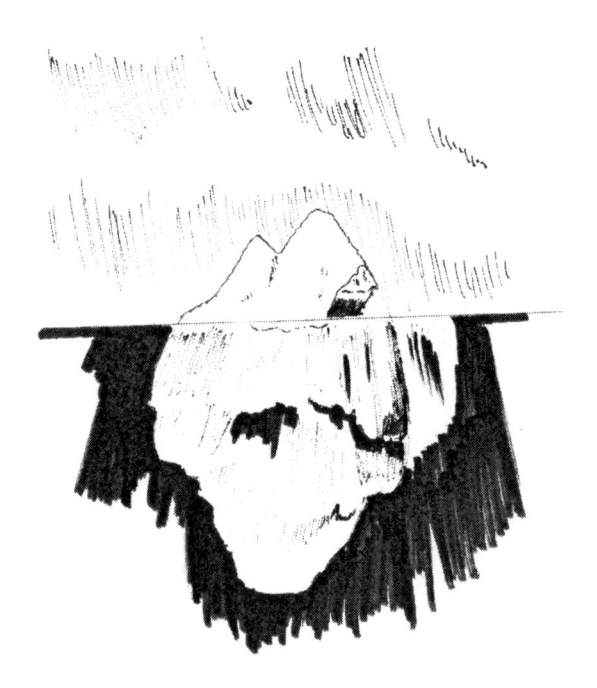

Beneath the Surface

If you want to get your head above the overwhelming sea of debt and deepen your understanding, then the following analogies will help you open your eyes to the issues that sit beneath the surface of the spending and shopping facade. Becoming aware that these issues exist will enable you to recognise and address them. As you get brave enough to delve beneath the surface, and face your fears, the iceberg will thaw out. As a result, your money and life will move in a healthier and wealthier direction, perhaps for the very first time ever. And on this voyage of discovery, you will find pearls of wisdom that literally change your whole life and perspective, for lessons learnt, reveal gems for us all.

I know this happened for me.

Budgeting - On its own, budgeting will not work for an emotional spender, as the urge to spend overpowers any logical stay at home budget sheet. How many times have you written a budget, but trampled on it on the way out of the door?

Consumerism - The word consume means to eat—consumerism is designed to eat your money fast, in as many ways as it can. And the more you feed it, the hungrier it gets!

Conventional Help - Gives a spendaholic the green light to go shopping! Financial advice, loans, and remortgaging do nothing to recognise or address emotional spending issues that built the debt, and hence the iceberg builds.

CREDit - Notice the word credit has *red* in it. Easy access to borrowing is lethal, especially if you've adopted the 'Oh, what the hell—I'll put it on the plastic' attitude.

My 1st Credit Card

I excitedly applied for my very first credit card, feeling like a proper grown-up. I remember the echoing words of my mate Mark, who was visiting on the day it arrived. 'Oh no, here comes trouble,' he remarked as I opened the letter addressed from Barclays. I remember my defensive response: 'No, Mark, I'm only going to use it when I really need to,' I quickly replied, as I shoved it in my purse.
'Yeah, I've heard that one before,' he replied.
I ignored the comments of this angel in disguise. But to this day, when I look back, I can hear his words loud and clear. A big part of me knew he was right, just as my mother had been many years before.
'Whatever you do, don't get a cheque book, use cash,' she advised. I ignored her wise words too.
Literally within an hour of receiving the Barclaycard, I was itching to see if it worked, so I jumped in the car, drove to the garage, and filled up with petrol, as easy as that. I'd gotten my first credit card buzz (or sting). If only I'd listened to my mother and Mark.

Hey Big Spender 'get an emotional grip'

> *Credit cards are consumer cocaine.*
> —John Cummuta

Over the years I ended up with a whole line in my purse!

Divorce - Over 70% of marriages end in divorce over money issues. One big problem is that couples rarely talk about money or sit down and regularly plan it. Also, once divorce is final, money problems can escalate, especially if you are the partner that never held the purse strings or managed the money.

Before Sharon's divorce, she'd never had to manage money. But once divorced, she was solely responsible for paying the mortgage and bills and providing for her son. The other problem was that Sharon had started using retail therapy to cheer herself up. She began to browse around the shops at lunchtimes and after work. On average, she was overspending by approximately £37.00 per week. With bank charges, this added up to over £2000 per year. If she fails to snap out of this habit, she could significantly incur huge debt and threaten her family's security in years to come.

Emotional Spending - Is used as outlets to express pent-up emotions such as loneliness, anger, and depression. Excitement and happiness can also entice people to spend a small fortune. Low moods are transformed to highs and more bubbly moods are creatively dispersed. The emotional shopping habit comes with a very high price tag attached. Maybe there is another meaning to the term '*high street*' after all? Emotional spending may seem the easy option, but it's not. No matter how many material possessions you buy, it will never be enough. You'll always want more, as shopping to feel good will never satisfy your true inner needs

Impulse Spending - This is when you react and buy a product or service moments after seeing it, which is precisely what consumerism is designed for you to do.

> *95% of people in UK, Australia, and America spend on impulse.*
> —John Cummuta

Lack of Money Education - Common-sense spending habits are not taught in schools, nor are lessons on how to get rich. I recommend Gill Fielding's book *Riches*; it explains rules of wealth that she believes everyone should know. Don't just leave wealth-building tools and rules to the rich!

No Plans - Failing to plan is the equivalent of getting in your car and not knowing where you're heading. You drive around in circles and use up all your fuel going nowhere. People prioritize shopping, family days out, weddings, holidays, parties, and funerals more than they plan their money! Except for rich people . . . *This is why they're rich!*

No Savings - No savings puts people in a scarcity mindset; there is always lack. And when money is needed in a crisis, it is borrowed with added interest. The simple rule is to save 10% of all money that comes in. That means you get to spend £900 out of every £1000.

Poor Beliefs - These are passed down through generations by parents and other family members, friends, religion, teachers, and the media. As you begin to recognise and change what you believe about money for the better, your new mindset can literally move mountains!

Self-Employed - Having a trade without knowing how to trade builds debt, especially if you're emotionally attached to your business. If you're in business with no vision and limited financial skills, this is a BIG problem.

Hey Big Spender 'get an emotional grip'

Risky Business

When I set up as a self-employed yoga teacher, I focused on being an excellent teacher, which I achieved; however, I failed to specifically plan, and this was my big downfall. I eventually had to cease doing that much-loved work.

When my spending addiction kicked in, it was when my classes were taking off. When times were good, over 120 people a week would attend the classes I had built from scratch. So in the early days of this success, I was generating the money to spend.

The BIG Gap - What's The BIG Gap between earning and spending money that many people fall down?

EARN_____?_____SPEND

Answer = <u>managing it</u>. Especially the emotions surrounding it!

As a working-class girl, I knew how to earn and how to spend money, but not how to manage it very well. Now I know different.

How much time do you spend managing and learning about money? Learn from the people who hit rock bottom and then made it to the top. Attend seminars on money, research online (many are free) and read great books such as *Think and Grow Rich*, by Napoleon Hill.

Retail Therapy - Shopping to feel good and boost your confidence distracts you for a while and makes you smile. Any habit is created by repeating a process often enough for it to become the norm.

A bit of retail therapy repeated again and again = an expensive and impulsive habit.

Spendaholism - Spendaholism to a spendaholic is what alcoholism is to an alcoholic, the only difference is that one person holds a bag and the other a bottle. Wikipedia states The word for compulsive desire to shop stems from the Greek word oniomania. Psychiatrists Bleuler (1924) and Kraepelin originally described oniomania over a century ago, they both include the syndrome in their early psychiatric text books. In the UK spendaholism remains practically unaddressed to this day.

Unemployment - Being unemployed can knock your confidence and cause money worries. No work or job loss equals more money going out than coming in. Perhaps lack of confidence around managing money prohibits you from moving forwards in a new career? Or maybe you've recently lost your job and need to adjust your lifestyle and spending habits? One thing you do have on your hands is time; learn to use it resourcefully.

Two Extremes - Two people I spoke to went out and blew a massive amount of money after losing their jobs. OTT I know but anything can happen when you hit the spending switch in an extreme emotional state.

1. The first person went on a £20,000 spending spree after losing a job in the forces.
2. The other person got extremely drunk after losing a high flying job. When he woke up the next morning there was a box on his desk. Inside was a £77,000 watch!

Abuse/Undervaluing Life Experiences - If you have been abused or mistreated in any way, either as a child or as an adult, this knocks your confidence and self-worth as a human being BIG time. The charity Refuge states that over 89% of women in abusive relationships have suffered some form of financial control. You may be shopping and overspending to distract yourself from the harsh reality of a certain situation or may fear facing it. There is no doubt that distraction does help to take your mind off your problems, but it is a double-edged sword if it builds debt in the process. Seeking the right type of help to deal with your situation professionally, when you are ready to face it, is best. See the references in the back of this book. Learning to be creative and to express yourself in constructive ways is also healing.

Hey Big Spender 'get an emotional grip'

*Find the inner strength to deal with your situation.
Don't let it build anymore.*

'I stayed in an abusive relationship because I had nowhere for my daughter and I to go. My partner told me that if I walked out, then it would be with nothing. This was scary. Eventually I did walk away, and despite very little material possessions, I had my sanity back. This felt priceless and was worth much more than the nice house and the flash car'.

—*Anon*

'Because of abuse I experienced in my teens, I never truly felt I was worthy of receiving money or a decent life as an adult. Whenever I had money, I would push it away or spend it until it disappeared. This then sent me back to survival mode. I suppose I didn't really believe that good things could happen to me . . . or I feared what may happen if they did'.

—*Anon*

'After going through domestic violence I was afraid to venture too far from my new safe address. I would only go as far as the corner shop for food and then head back home. Because of the amount of money this was costing, often by Friday I would have no money left for utilities, and on many occasions, I would sit in the dark over the weekend. When I realised the extent of what this pattern was costing me, I got brave enough to face my fears. I took a confidence course and ventured out and do a proper shop. I felt empowered and for the first time began to save'.

—*Anon*

Ann Carver

Melt or Build

Depending on what you reach out for in your vulnerable moments will determine if you the iceberg will melt or build. Circle the words that will make your situation better and cross out the words that will make your situation worse;

Alcohol / Talking / Getting the right help / Shopping / Drugs / Creativity

What's beneath your iceberg?

Spend a few moments reflecting on the underlying issues that may have enabled your spending habits to build.

> *A pearl is created by a grain of sand that embeds itself in an oyster's shell. The sand irritates the oyster, so it sprays the inside of its shell with a smooth and sticky liquid that protects it. The sand rolls around in the sticky liquid. As layer upon layer builds, it creates a pearl.*

The moral of this analogy is that pearls exist in your money / life crisis—if you take action to transform them

3

Get Change

This part of the book is comprised of tools, strategies, and metaphors for you to change the way you spend and behave around money. You can work through it in whichever order you chose. 'Get Change' gives you the power to break through any roadblocks in the forms of fears and personal challenges, whether it's your own fears or outside influences that stand in your way and attempt to stop you moving your money and life forwards.

Often you can be your own worst enemy as far as managing money is concerned. Your destructive patterns of behaviour have been rooted and established over a long period. As you begin to pave a new way forwards, the old you will naturally want to put up a resistance; however, get change enables you to combat and overcome such challenges.

Safe Spending like Safe Sex?

Realistically, can change happen? The answer is *yes*, it can. Just as people have learnt to have safe sex, people can also learn to spend safely! Like safe sex, you just need to put the correct protection mechanisms in place as far as you and your spending habits are concerned. Talking about money issues to me is the new *'coming out'*. Up until the credit crunch, people in the UK have been more open about their sexuality than their relationship with money. So confessing about money surely has to be the next BIG thing to come out of the closet.

Coming out about my own debt and life situation has been liberating beyond measure and has led me to my destiny. The moment I came clean was the moment my journey to true freedom begun from the inside out. First I became emotionally free as my pent-up self learnt to release. Yes, it began with tears, but these watered the seeds to grow me. Then my mind began to clear, and I could look toward a brighter future—and that's when the magic happened and reality became a great place to be.

The Power of Money

Money's an extremely powerful source, not to be reckoned with. When used emotionally in the wrong way, it builds more trouble than it's worth and can affect us in ways you didn't bargain for. For some people, no amount of money ever satisfies or seems enough; others don't feel worthy of receiving it and self-sabotage it the minute it comes their way. Yet when money is used emotionally in the right way, it can bring much joy, happiness, and stability. Learn feel good about it and treat it well and the odds will definitely stack in your favour.

Emotional Spending Triggers Points

The following list describes intense emotional states that send you on a spending spree, to either express or to help distract yourself from facing the full impact of your feelings.

Anger - Spending in a rage will prove very expensive. Also be careful *not* to take your mood out on any shop assistant. Learn to express your anger is constructive and less expensive ways other than spending money.

Anxiety - Expensive mistakes are often anxious buys. Stop grabbing for items. Take a few deep breaths and shop with calm and control.

Bereavement - Shopping to fill in an empty space after the loss of a loved one can be healing, as it distracts you for a short while, but this antidote soon wears off. Don't get in debt attempting to cover up your feelings, as it'll make matters worse, not better. I recommend going to bereavement counselling, as you'll find solace from people who aren't attached to your situation but can empathise with you. It takes approximately two years for the intenseness to lift, so go easy on you.

Boredom - Tania refuses to shop weekly. She doesn't drive and is home all day with the kids. The highlight of the day is getting her husband to take her shopping after work. Together they spend a small fortune. Boredom is a state of mind that will zap your money.

Competition - Linda shops on eBay and will outbid others for the sheer competition of not wanting anyone else to have that handbag!

Confidence - This comes from the inside, not from yet another new dress. Courage brings confidence, so be brave.

Crisis - Reaching out to the shop shelves in times of crisis will only add to your money troubles. Reach out for the right help, but resist reaching out to the material world until your crisis is over!

Depression - Look up, not down. Step outside of yourself. Do something for someone else. Take an uphill walk and climb to the top, step by step.

Excitement - Get excited about saving money NOT spending it

Guilt and Shame - Buying to make up for how you feel or have behaved will soon be noticed by others. Be careful, as they may get you to guilt buy more often that you think!

Happiness - Is free, it cannot be bought. What does happiness mean to you? What makes you really smile?

Insecurity - Securing a bargain or yet another dodgy deal is *not* the answer!

Jealousy - It will cost you a fortune if you buy out of spite

Loneliness - Shopping takes you to where people are. Perhaps you don't visit the shops solely to buy things but to meet with people? What can you do to socialise more?

Love - Learn to love keeping your money, more than spending it.

Worry - A common breakdown by psychologists of time we spend on different kinds of worry is as follows;

> 40% of worry is over things that will never happen *(you will never run out of clothes!)*
> 30% of worry is about what happened in the past *(buying the wrong size)*
> 12% is over unnecessary health concerns *(it might make me sick)*
> 10% is over petty and miscellaneous cares *(what others may think of me)*
> Just 8% is real and justified!

How do you get an emotional grip?

Getting to grips with the emotions that keep packing you off on a shopping trip is the golden key that will put you back in control and empower you to keep more of your money.

First acknowledge the fact that your behaviour is costing you great pain. The buzz has become a heavy burden. Just suppose for a moment that you carried on your spending habits for the next year. How would you feel? How about the next five years? Look at the mess are you in now and reflect how it may have affected your life and your relationships. How about if you continued to recklessly spend for another ten years? Yes, I know it hurts, but I want you to see that bad things can happen, to hopefully snap you out of it.

People move away from pain and towards pleasure. Up until now, you've been connecting to the pleasure that overspending has bought you, such as the buzz of buying spontaneously and from the joy of seeing people's faces light up every time you surprise them. You did not bargain for the pain, such as debt, despair, and addiction to shopping, that would follow, did you?

Tony is in debt because he adores the attention he gets from women when he splashes out on champagne in night clubs. Yet he yearns to have his wife and family back. He is also aware that his destructive behaviours caused the break-up, but he refuses to stop.

Better patterns of behaviour create much better habits.

Wealth Seminar

I left the 'Wealth Mastery' seminar in the most optimistic state I'd felt in years. With my new 'I can do attitude' I believed that debt freedom was possible. What was the reason for this? Because the knowledge I learnt about me and money that day was worth its weight in gold. I especially was inspired by people who had gone broke and then made a decision that the only way was up. I knew I could achieve debt freedom if I put my mind to it and rolled my sleeves up. Just as I had created my financial mess, I could equally reverse tactics. Knowing I had the power to achieve made me want to take responsibility and snapped my out of procrastination. Prior to the event, I remember being wary and pessimistic. I told the organizer who called me 'there was no way I could afford to go', to which he replied, 'you can't afford not to.' My gut instincts knew he was right, so I gave him and myself the benefit of the doubt and signed up, thank goodness.

Benefits of Change

Spending money is part of our modern culture, and unless we head off to the wilderness, there's no escaping this fact. However, growth comes when we can choose to spend money in ways that will benefit us. One big lesson I learnt from this experience is that spending time learning about money and behaviour change is a great investment. Whether you're researching on line, watching tele-seminars, learning from role-models, visiting the library or attending live seminars (much better than any music gig). Money education in the UK and parenting skills concerning this crucial subject are extremely limited in conventional education, however with the World Wide Web all learning is accessible. So once, I'd spent my money right, as the 'Wealth Mastery' event changed how I ticked on the inside. And it has continued to improve my performance and be extraordinarily life changing.

I hope that by reading this, your eyes open wide to the endless possibilities the moment you decide to change. Behaviour change techniques will enable you to get your head up and above any overwhelming situations by helping you to recognise and break through the many excuses and fears of the mind that hold you back.

- Have you ever found yourself wanting to desperately change, but then the voice from within tells you not to bother or says that you're not capable?
I hope strategies in this book move you beyond any such fibs.

> *When you're in recovery, you soon begin to
> realise that the fears you were once afraid of facing
> aren't really that big.*
>   —Angie V

Belief System

A business lady was visiting from Poland; she was astounded that as a nation we are not taught about money from childhood. As a child, she was encouraged to account for every penny she earned and spent. She had to write this down twice. One copy was for her and the other for her parents. She has grown up with excellent money management skills and still uses this method today.

Blaming your parents or failed education is equally unhealthy, and if you're not careful, this will become an excuse not to bother. The best thing to do is agree, for the better of your wealth, to commit to learning new tricks and to taking responsibility for your money and life. Gill Fielding, author of *Riches*, associated growing up in a poor environment with the need to do well. Her first job was as an accountant, and to this day, money fascinates her. She loves money and is proud of saying it. So bad experiences can turn out to be blessings in disguise, for they help you to define what you don't want out of life.

Re-connecting

Often it's as if we have been wired to spend and we need re-wiring. For example, my love for shopping started at an early age. Shopping with my parents made me happy. Being out in public together meant they would be on their best behaviour, as when they were at home behind closed doors they did nothing but argue, so when they were happy I was happy too. Also as a teenager, my best friend and I loved to visit Camberley Town at weekends. Our parents gave us quite a generous allowance to spend on new clothes; we loved trying them on and buying clothes that matched. Together, both events established a strong connection of loving shopping as they related to significant times in my childhood that were happy and involved my parents and my best friend. Home life as a child was unhappy as my father was shell shocked after the war and fuelled his torment with alcohol, so this time spent at the shops were valuable to me.

A few years later, my parents divorced, and my allowance ended. Any money I wanted from now on had to be earned. I found this tough at the time but set to work, as the thought of having no money took my freedom and quality time out with my friends away.

In my adult years, my shopping habit spiralled out of control, for my happy connection with shopping became my solace or make up in tough times. Looking back now, it's a shame I wasn't wired to save part of my allowance. Yes I did have a post office savings book, but never dreamed of stopping there on my way to town. If I could re-wind and put just 10% in that little blue book, so out of every £10, I could have saved £1 and spent £9 and kept putting 10% of my wages away in my adult years. If I had, I'd have grown up rich!

Defining Moment

Behaviour change techniques raised my awareness to where my habits and behaviours around money originally evolved. Although I can explain and write about these now, I wasn't conscious of these facts when I was in the heart of my spending problem. This newfound awareness changed me big time. I now realised that the mess I had gotten myself into, I could equally get out of. This defining moment enabled me to make a conscious decision that my bad spending habits were going to change for better ones. I can honestly say this was the turning point for me, and it proved to be life changing.

To sum this up in my terms; I believe that money's like water: it flows in and flows out. It's up to you and I to govern the inflow and outflow of our money, just as the moon governs the ebb and flow of the tide. The secret is to manage your money in ways that create abundant waves of wealth. If you have a clear and wealthy destination in mind, then even the most turbulent and unpredictable waters will keep you carrying on in the mightiest of storms. This is a universal law called *cause and effect*, as every action has a reaction. What thoughts, acts, and deeds you give out will come back to you. However 'no captain ever learnt to sail a ship in calm waters', so if you got off to a bad start with your money and life, know that you can learn to reset the sail and change the direction of your destiny. What's gone is gone. It's what you do now that will determine where you end up, and the sooner you start, the better, for the murky waters will soon become clearer.

Money will give you the respect you deserve, if you treat it with value and respect. Money flows to the people who treat it well; it is entrusted to those who deserve it. *Dragons' Den* investors will only invest their money in people who will value and respect their money, as they know they will get their money back with interest. Yet if you treat it with negligence, abuse, and disrespect, it'll soon flow away from you. When this happens, it isn't bad luck but a result of bad management. However, the slightest change you make for good will have a ripple effect that will reach a turning point and come flowing back.

Enough was Enough

I clearly remember the day I decided that enough was enough. Desperate and in debt, I wanted my life to change because I couldn't stand the intense pressure anymore. I hated receiving phone calls and letters, the humiliation of having to say that I couldn't pay. Even worse was when I had to say no the kids. In the beginning, I thought I'd be able to handle my debts, but they grew much bigger. I felt angry with myself for getting in such a mess, and I wanted to be debt-free. The sheer thought of thinking enough was enough began a ripple effect.

After this definite decision of wanting to be debt-free, I noticed doors of opportunities opening for me. My outlook was changing. Instead of seeking solace in shopping, I was setting my sail towards debt freedom. The moment I wanted to be debt-free, my life's ripple effects went as follows:

The Advert I walked into a newsagent and saw an advert that read, 'Train to be a life coach'. I liked the idea of learning to set goals and moving on with my life. I signed up, and the investment and commitment paid off . . .

Just the Ticket As a thank you for enrolling, The Coaching Academy sent me a free ticket to a seminar called 'Unleash the Power Within', with one of the world's number one coaches, Anthony Robbins. The four-day seminar is designed to enable people to transform fear into power by inviting them to recognise, uncover, and use the most powerful resources that we already possess - courage, faith, determination and passion—in order to grow, contribute, and celebrate at the deepest, most powerful level. When I arrived at the ExCel centre in London, I had no idea what to expect, but my intentions were to grasp this opportunity with both hands. Over ten thousand people from all lifestyles and diverse backgrounds attended the life-changing event. When it ended, I felt as if could move mountains.

Next I attended 'Wealth Mastery' and discovered the great work of John Cummuta's Transforming Debt to Wealth Programme, which I followed. Conventional help had calculated that it would take me twelve years to pay my debts back, but John's strategy challenged that and said it would take me seven. Deep down, I wanted to pay them off quicker. I followed his plan for a while, until yet another opportunity presented itself and I was able to pay them back in three years!

Better Habits On the first trip to the shops after the seminar, I checked my kitchen cupboards, took a smaller trolley once I arrived, and adjusted my posture (as if I were going into battle). I said to myself, *Today I am saving myself a fortune and getting from the entrance to the exit with no excess baggage!* Every time I felt temptation pull, I pulled back. Any unnecessary items that did land in my trolley, I put back. And if any such items did strangely make it to the till, I told the cashier that I did not want them. *Check me out!* To my amazement, when I went to pay, my bill was down by one-third of what I typically spent! I drove home with a smile on my face and a sense of control. I thought to myself, *this is a credit to me . . . and* not *the retailer.*

Ownership The moment I stopped shopping to find solace and began to take a look into my inner life, was when I began to recognise the specific points where things had gone wrong—and where I had used shopping to try to put them right. Finally, I was taking ownership (owning my ship).

Professional Help I also got professional help to deal with my past, and gradually I let go of the guilt and shame that I realised I'd been carrying around for most of my adult life, self-sabotaging over events that started when I was a child! It was time to become truly free.

Local Appreciation My husband and I decided we'd have no more holidays for at least three years. Instead, we decided to walk and explore our local area. This in itself was enriching, as we grew to love and appreciate living on the beautiful South Coast of England, where up until now we had taken in for granted. We found a new sense of appreciation, and to this day, we still love to walk and ride bikes regularly in our area. Each time, we discover new paths we'd previously never seen.

It Didn't Stop There One particular day we were walking along the shore from Langstone to Emsworth and discussing our financial situation. We were contemplating moving house to free up money to pay our debts off more quickly. Ten minutes later, we'd arrived at the town and were looking in an estate agent's window. 'May I help you?' a voice enquired.

It was the estate agent, and later that day, he came to look at our house. His first reaction was that our garden was big enough to sell as a building plot! It took a while, but a year or so later, it sold for £66,000.

Honouring Debts I wanted to honour the debts I had created, although in order to keep the creditors at bay, I did have to go on a debt management programme until the land sold. However, as soon as the money was in the bank, the debts were paid back. Personally, for me, this was an important part of my healing process of becoming truly debt-free.

Writing I began to write about my journey of debt freedom and the methods that had helped me along the way, for me this was a healthy and less expensive way to express

The Ripple Effect Continued Then the social entrepreneur school had arrived for the first time in Portsmouth and was interviewing potential candidates. I took my manuscript and my passion along and was awarded a place.

> Unfortunately the standard of education systems of most countries and normal upbringing will generally destroy the sense of wonder because a big part of society think that money or the appreciation of it is distasteful, downgrading or evil.
> —Gill Fielding

Don't Be Scared, Be Brave

- Are you scared of money?
- Have you never been taught how to nurture, love, and respect it?
- Were you raised believing that loving money is wrong or even evil?

Decide to take the lead over your money, be the master of it. Don't be scared to love your money, as it'll be scared of you. Not that money has any feelings. Money doesn't care what you do with it. You can choose to love it, abuse it, spend it, steal it, or do great things with it. However, if you're scared of money, you'll find yourself mismanaging it and avoiding facing it. Consequently, you will never have enough, you'll never build wealth, and you will never truly appreciate what you have. You will wealth sabotage! So learn to develop a healthy relationship with your money and watch as it responds differently. The more you love and respect your money, the more it will decide to hang around. Spending less than you earn is a way of showing your money tender loving care. Loving and looking after what you have will bring a good return.

Can fear of money be a good thing?

Fear of overspending, getting in debt, or gambling it all away are good fears, as they act as protection mechanisms. Fear of not being able to pay for things on credit can be enough to make you decline it.

> 'To be without some of the things you want is an indispensable part of happiness'
> —Bertrand Russell

Can living in fear of money be a bad thing?

Fear of not having enough (or lack) can trigger you to react in ways that get you in big debt. Some people will beg, borrow, and steal to ensure they have enough. Fearlessness of money and adopting the 'have to have it now attitude' to fulfil self-gratification is a dangerous and expensive habit to adopt, especially with credit cards, loans, and payday loan companies They prey on borrowers because they know how much they can earn in interest, so they dish out money as if it's candy.

> *Love and fear are the same but different. They are both strong feelings. The difference is in the experience. Some humans fear to live in love and others love to live in fear!*

Any unhealthy fears you hold about money can be overcome. What do you fear about money? Perhaps you're scared that you'll never have enough or you fear losing it all. What if any of these things really do happen? Then what? What will you gain out of the experience? Perhaps the momentum to have another go, and make it work better the next time? Learn to build a better loving relationship with your money. Look at it in the same way that you were taught to swim or ride a bike. It may take a few attempts, but the more you practice, the better you'll get. If you mess up, don't lose heart. Face your fears and keep improving and building on your skills.

> *You have nothing to lose, just lots to gain.*

The Flip Side of the Coin

The opposite of fear is love. Overcome fear by learning to love money. Know that fears will always appear, as that's life. Even if you are flat broke, you can begin to mend your money by reading and researching from other people who have conquered financial adversity. Visit the library and pick up books such as Paul McKenna's *I Can Make You Rich,* Brendon Berchard's *The Secret Millionaire or Think and Grow Rich* by Napoleon Hill. Go online and research a wealth of information with the likes of Brian Tracy and John Cummuta. Play motivation and educational CDs in your car; transform it into your classroom on wheels and drive your money and life forwards in a more confident way. Become a sponge to learning and you'll be surprised at how fascinating money and life becomes. And use the strategies in this book.

Relationship

Your relationship with money can often seem like a distant friendship or one that didn't last or get off to a good start. You attempt to communicate with it—but within the limited ways you know. If only you'd been encouraged to cherish your relationship with money from the word go. The key for any happy relationship is love and trust. Learning to love and nurture your money enables it to grow in ways that will boost and enhance your relationship with it. As you learn to pay attention to it, look after it, and listen to it, this can also create much wealth (providing you with a sense of well-being).

6 Steps to Get Change

1. **Decide to love it** - Gill Fielding, author of *Riches*, says this: *Even as a child living 'financially poor' in the back streets of London, I knew how to make money and I knew it instinctively. I assumed that everybody knew how to make money, they just chose not to.* Loving money and life is key, no matter how little or how much you have.
2. **Serve money well** - Money is like any other relationship: learn to serve it well. However, ignore the signs and you'll be its slave!
3. **Pay attention** - If you don't love something, it's easy to turn your back on it. When opportunities do come, you don't see them.
4. **Gratitude and appreciation** - Whatever amount of money comes your way, accept it with an attitude of appreciation. Nowadays I say thank you for every single penny that comes my way, and this sense of appreciation enables me to cherish it. I also say thank you to the amount of money I will one day receive.

5. **Receive it** - Learn to receive and accept the money that comes your way. Stand with your arms open wide and know that you are worthy of receiving in abundance.
6. **Believe** - Whatever money skills you lack, believe that you can learn them. Know that money skills are learnt in the same way that you learn to drive a car. Believe you can also get very good at it, for it is easier than we are led to believe. The financial world can purposely complicate the simplest of task, because they don't want you to know their best-kept secrets.

Say the following: *'I love money, and money loves me. We respect and care for each other from this day onwards, forever and ever'.*

4

RED The Spending Pirate

It's time to introduce you to RED the Spending Pirate. RED adores spending your money. You may not know it, but RED has been tempting you to part with your cash for a lot longer than you realise. RED knows that up until now, winning you over has been as easy job for him, as you are in the habit of buying first and thinking last, regardless of whether you can afford to or not.

RED the Spending Pirate is a metaphor, like a character in a game. He is specially designed to help you snap out of your spending habits and recognise your own personal pirate behaviour. You will soon be left with more money and feel happier for it, as you wise up and begin to play RED's money game to your advantage. Although RED is only a make believe character, the effects of him on your money and life are very real. RED means danger, overdrawn at the bank debt, the colour of seduction and STOP.

- What's the difference between a real pirate and RED?

A real pirate robs ships, but RED robs you of your money and happiness!

RED History

As a woman, I knew I had to seriously rein my spending habits in. But at the same time I couldn't just stop emotional shopping as I'd got accustomed to it and loved it too much. Also being a woman, there are always food and essentials to buy, genuine bargains to be had and needs for the kids. So to tell myself *'I was never going to over shop or overspend again'* was definitely unrealistic. But at the same time I knew I needed a powerful strategy to enable me to shop with savvy and control, but to also have fun in the process. That's when I created 'RED the Spending Pirate', each and every time I went shopping I pretended I was competing in a game and I was determined to win. The aim of the game was to get to be <u>fully aware</u> of when RED was tempting me to buy unwanted items or ridiculous things and to tell him to 'walk the plank' (or go do one), before I parted with my money. This was especially powerful in times when I found I was easily distracted, such as when I was out shopping with the kids or in my weak and hyped-up moments of stress (especially with PMS)! To my pleasant surprise my game plan worked, as I soon began to outsmart him and line my own treasure chest! I felt empowered. *Yippee!!*

On my first trip to the shops with RED in mind, my shopping bill reduced by approx a third! I drove home feeling the most empowered I had felt that day. Also it wasn't long before my youngest daughter mastered it. On week three of my new shopping regime she said *'mummy can I have'* . . . . suddenly her words stopped in mid air, she then turned and looked me straight in the eye and said *'don't tell me your sticking to your plan and outsmarting that pirate'!* Another thing I noticed was that my kids had pirates too, as up until this defining moment the words *'mum can I have'* were asked many times.

RED Reflection

RED is a reflection of;

1. That little devil side of your personality that entices you to spend almost every day, of every week of every year.
2. The outside influences that pull on your wallet and purse strings, such as consumerism, loan companies, sales people and anyone else, such as family and friends that tug on your wallet and purse and make money disappear from your bank as if by magic!

As you get to know RED, you'll be shocked at the many ways he's been seducing you to spend spend spend. As you open your eyes to this fact, you'll learn to build your *NO* muscle and ignore his naughty and expensive behaviour, and you'll even start to laugh at the many pathetic temptations that he tries to puts in your path. And your wallet and purse will get fatter for it too, because the less spent on RED, the more money you'll have left for you.

Remember, every time you tell RED to take a splash, you will be left with less debt and more cash. The RED side of your personality is easily tempted to overspend, especially when you;

- Shop with your eyes shut, especially when you're tired or in a rush
- Spend money because you feel excited, depressed or lonely
- Are in the habit of looking for a quick fix to feel good
- Are enticed to spend by like-minded spendthrifts

Seduced by RED

Have you had the equivalent to RED tugging on your wallet/purse strings?

- Are you easily tempted into buying what you didn't plan?
- Do you find yourself saying yes when you really mean to say NO?

Consumerism is designed for you to spend your money in as many ways as it can. It knows the RED side of your behaviour simply can't resist. And the more you give in to consumerists' way of thinking, the easier it is for them to have control over you, because every emotional and impulse purchase builds a habit. You can often be tricked into buying items you thought you would like, but didn't intend to buy, especially when you're in need of a pick-me-up, in fact you may as well write EASY WITH MONEY or I'LL SAY YES TO ANYTHING in BIG letters across your forehead. But know that each time you emotionally or impulsively spend, you're allowing yourself to be seduced by consumerism at your expense!

The word cREDit has *RED* in it!

RED's a reflection of you when you spend like you do. I'm sure you already know him well! RED patiently waits to hook the vulnerable side of you into buying the next item and the next! RED doesn't care how fragile your finances are—or the amount of debt you are in. Seriously, RED is a danger to your future money and happiness, as he plans to drain every penny from your possession and more! When your money runs out, RED knows you will access more. I hope as a result of reading this you're beginning to see RED!!

Tempting RED

Just switch on the TV shopping channel, log onto the Internet, or simply step over the threshold of a shop and RED is there right by your side, as happy as can be. He especially loves the superstores and shopping precincts, where your senses go wild with tastes, sights, sounds, delicious smells, and new clothes to try on. RED can easily tempt you in every aisle you turn down. RED especially loves:

- Designer brands and latest trends
- Toys (toy cars and real ones), games, and gadgets of every kind
- BOGOF offers, bargains and sales
- Dining out for breakfast, dinner, and lunch
- Splashing out on pamper time, especially going on holiday
- Scratch cards, gambling and lottery
- When you go shopping for a few items and check out with a trolley full

RED knows that waiting for birthdays or Christmas is an outdated thing to do. He knows you like to pretend it's your birthday at least 17 times a year! The RED part of your personality continues to want more and more, as it's very rarely satisfied.

Seeing RED

At first RED tempts you to spend on affordable items that bring you instant gratification, such as making a grab for chocolate, fast food and treating yourself to clothes you can justifiably afford. At soon as he knows the shopping bug has bit, he will aim to stretch you towards desiring bigger and better things. Shopping makes RED jump with glee, as he loves turning heads and getting attention from others. He also adores it when you wine and dine in restaurants and cafes—and especially when you spontaneously book a holiday. Tempting you to spend is like food for RED's ego.

Guarantee that RED

- Is out to rob you blind
- Loves it when you flash the cash
- Tempts you to spend, regardless of whether you can afford it or not
- Is nearby patiently waiting every time you shop, and
- Gets you in mountains of debt and distress

Listen to RED Whisper

RED is difficult to see but easy to hear. However, the more you get to know him, the easier it is to spot him. Listen for RED's persuasive talk. Notice him whispering in your ear as you go through your daily chores;

'Go on—you deserve it'
'Let's pop to the shop'
'Oh don't be so tight'
'You have nothing to wear'
'The latest models better, yours is outdated'
'But you are buying it for someone else'
'The woman up the road has one and she earns less than you'

RED *Especially* Loves

- Cash point machines & credit cards
- Christmas, birthdays, valentine's day, mother's day, father's day etc
- Celebrations (especially weddings) and spontaneity
- When you buy out of guilt
- And demanding kids!

RED also loves it when your money runs dry and when you borrow more, as the more you spend, the richer he gets.

Hey Big Spender 'get an emotional grip'

RED *Especially* Hates

- The word *NO*
- Budgeting and planning your future
- Credit cards that get cut up
- When you generally keep a tight ship
- When you take time to shop calmly and think about what you buy
- The thought of your outsmarting him, as he knows the tide will turn in your favour and not his.

RED Fact

RED will drain your money and your happiness and pass your spending habits down to your kids. Answer the following questions:

- *Has RED been part of your for life longer than you realise Yes / No?*
- *Does RED have more control over your money than you have Yes / No?*

RED's Little Secret

RED knows that what you're truly searching for can never be bought or found on any shop shelf. For the real treasures in life, such as happiness and fulfilment, are found from the inside out, *not* the outside in, like nuggets of gold and pearls. RED's hidden this secret from you for as long as he could, as he's fully aware that the moment you find out about his antics, will be the moment you start playing the game to your advantage. And your money and life situation will have a fairy-tale ending.

- Do you want to let RED continue to rob you and possibly end up paying for the rest of your life?
  Or
- Do you want to outsmart RED and *strike gold?*

RED's Advantage

If you shop because you're stressed or depressed, RED knows he has an advantage over you. He knows you'll be easy prey. But know that he cannot force you into buying anything without your permission. If you shop because you are feeling sad, know that the debt you will end up with will make you sadder. If you simply don't know how money works, then start by spending less than you earn and be willing to learn. If you shop because you are bored, then find something more fulfilling to do in your spare time. You never know, one day your creativity may even make you money. Know that <u>you can</u> chose to spend your money and time in more fulfilling and wealthier ways other than shopping and blowing it all.

Focus on *You*, NOT RED

The secret to this is simple, learn to focus on what <u>you want</u>, not what RED desires. If you want more money, resist buying added extras. If you want to be debt-free, say no to all forms of borrowing and keep your hands in your pockets. If you want to stop acting like a spoilt brat, start acting more like a grown-up. Learn to internally switch off to all ads that tempt you to flash the cash or card. Quit all unplanned spending sprees, as this mode of thinking will cost you your dreams. Get to know what you want out of your money and life (more on this in the chapter 'Vision & Goals') and begin to dismiss all temptations that wait in your path by politely telling RED where to get off! Know that you will never change consumerism, but you can change how you respond to it. The more you think, plan and map out your journey, the more RED will shrink small.

RED Warning

Red is a danger to your future money and happiness.

Hey Big Spender 'get an emotional grip'

The Money Mast

Look at the different characters on the money mast and then answer the following questions:

1. Which one reflects your relationship with money at this moment in time? Why is this?
2. Now define where you would ideally like to be on the money mast. Why is this?

5

RED Dot Shopping

Designed for you reduce your weekly spending up to a third!

I had no idea of how much money I was wasting. All I knew was that it ran out fast. After one week of RED Dot shopping, *I had £100 left.*
Michelle H

RED Dot Shopping is powerful and brand-new way to shop that will save you an absolute fortune week by week, as long as you are determined to tell RED to get lost.

Know the more you put it into practice the easier it will get, just the same as when you first learnt to drive a car. Know that just as your emotional and impulsive spending habits were established, they can also be undone with RED Dot Shopping.

RED-Dot shopping is a unique *Hey Big Spender strategy* that enables you to do the following:

- £ Find out just how much RED is costing you.
- £ Change your day to day spending habits for the better.
- • Would you like to reduce your weekly spending by approx a third?

Ann Carver

Habits can be good or bad RED Dot shopping is an excellent habit to adopt.

The first time I put RED Dot Shopping into practice, I was determined to get from the start to the finish of my shopping trip with a lot more money left than I normally would. I drove home feeling empowered. I love being the one in control when I go out shopping. It's as if I am crediting me instead of the retailer!

RED Dot Shopping is especially useful to keep your spending on track in your most vulnerable moments, such as spending when excited, tired, depressed, stressed, or when the kids are pulling on your wallet/purse strings.

Use RED Dot Shopping while out shopping, Online, browsing TV channels, in your business, or in any other part of your life where you're tempted to emotionally or impulse spend.

Red Dot Shopping Instructions

You will need a red pen and a calculator.

1. Shop as you normally shop for one week BUT keep every single receipt
2. At the end of the week, you will need 15 minutes of your time and the receipts you have collected. With the red pen put a RED Dot by
- Every penny you did not intend to spend
- Every item you did not intend to buy

Now go through every receipt and repeat Dot Dot Dot

3. NOW add up ALL the Red Dots =£ ....
This is how much your pirate spending behaviour has cost you just for this week!
Are you shocked or not?

Bread	1.20
Washing Powder	5.70
Tomatoes	0.78
DVD	12.00●
Computer Ink	21.00
CD	8.99●
Milk	1.40
Pizza	3.70
Butter	1.50
Rice	2.70
Red Wine	9.99
Sirloin Steak	10.80●
Coffee	3.99
Chocolate	3.70
Dress	30.00
Shoes	27.00●
Shampoo	3.00
Dog food	7.00
Dog treats	3.00●
Oranges	2.20
Sweets	2.85
Potatoes	3.95
Ready meals	10.00
Toy car	15.00
Book	8.99
Paracetomol	1.20
Crisps	4.50
Chicken	7.99
Total	£ 214.13
	RED DOTS =£61.79

Hey Big Spender 'get an emotional grip'

4. Now multiply the RED Dot total by 52 to see how much RED costs you over 1 year.
   =£ ....
   Yes you're spending may vary from week to week, but many of your spending patterns have become habitual. So this gives you a rough idea.
5. NOW divide the yearly figure by 12 to see how much RED costs you a over month
   =£ ....
6. For a 3 year reality check, multiply the yearly figure by 3
   =£ ....

At this point Linda said 'OMG this is a holiday in Ibiza!

Now you know roughly how much your spending habits are costing you **STOP** and think twice the next time you are tempted by RED. **REMEMBER** the RED Dot the next time you shop and **STOP RESIST & WALK AWAY**. Each and every time you do will be CREDIT YOU!

Aim to build and strengthen your NO muscle week by week. Set yourself a goal to reduce your spending by at from 10%-25% or more, so you behave and save yourself a fortune week by week. What could you do with all that money instead?

My weekly spending was;

Week 1 £ ....
Week 2 £ ....
Week 3 £ ....
Week 4 £ ....

RED Dot Shopping kits are available to purchase at www.heybigspenders.co.uk

Contents include; receipt wallet, distraction band, red dot pen, spending intentions pad, red dot sticker, 12 track CD (includes coming to your senses relaxation)

What other RED Dot Shoppers have said:

> *Now I am saving £50 a week.* —Susie T

> *The first time I grasped this simple concept, I felt empowered*
> —Lizzy Sands

> RED Dot Shopping *helped me to stop and think. I can now go into a shop and resist against buying on impulse and this feels good.* —Susan H.

Kate Kendal, has a good job in London, she measured her impulse spending and realized it was totalling approximately £200 per week. That's over £10,000 per year! She's now investing 50% in refurbishing her flat.

Lisa didn't see herself as a massive spender; she didn't even like shopping. Her husband's a builder and likes a good hearty meal and a big packed lunch to take to work. Once a week, they visit the superstore to stock up. Because of red-dot shopping, this is what Lisa said:

> Red dot shopping *made me realise that for the past twelve years, at least one-third of the items that I have been putting in the trolley have been trash! The ironic thing also is that I have been in debt for the same amount of time! Not only did I spend £47 less in the first week, but I went home and made cakes with the kids. They loved it! I'm now shopping with my eyes open and putting £40 a week in an unbreakable pot. If I find myself breaking it to get the money out, then I will know my spending is worse than I thought. I can use this extra money to bring my debts down and maybe even have a holiday.*

Pressure Pot

Julie has disabled twin daughters and goes shopping to take the pressure off in tough times. Julie will shop regardless if she has the money or not, so often gets in debt over it, which is even more worrying for her. Once she realised what retail therapy was costing her, she decided to save money especially for her pressure release. She calls her savings her pressure pot. She says she feels empowered, is able to say no and prefers to shop less. Her daughters are also saving too.

7 Benefits of RED Dot shopping

1. Fattens your wallet and purse
2. Puts you in control
3. Enables you to focus on what you really want
4. Builds your *no* muscle day by day.
5. Rubs off on the partner and kid(s)
6. Installs wealthier habits
7. Empowers you beyond measure

Don't try to tempt me Shopping.
I'm sticking to the list

6

Dealing with RED

Now you've got to know RED and how much he is costing you, it's time for you to deepen your understanding of your very own pirate behaviour and highlight your spending traits, so you can stop RED in his tracks. Know this is absolutely key to plugging your spending leaks and refilling the wallet / purse. Just as you're spending habits were created by your desire to shop and spend, know your wallet / purse can fatten with your desire to be richer, more confident and happier. This chapter should prove to be an empowering process for you and your money.

Altogether there are 14 steps to take. The first 7 will explore you and you're spending at its very worst. The following 7 will explore the potential of what brand new habits can do for you once RED has walked the plank.

- Do you want to change your pirate spending habits for wealthier ones?
- Are you ready to break free from the hypnotic effect that RED has on you?

Note of reassurance: *Finding RED will lead you to the PEARLS*

Part One—7 Steps to Recognise RED in YOU

1 - Be Willing

The following sentence is for you to state that you are willing to explore how RED's behaviour is affecting you, even if you think you already know, completing this exercise will open your eyes even more.

Complete the following sentence;

I (*your name*),... am willing to explore my RED behaviour.

Success is the ability to breakthrough

2 - The Place—Where are you when you spend like you do?

It's crucial for you pinpoint exactly where you physically are when your spending is at its worst. Then you will be more aware of where RED waits to tempt you.

- Where are you when RED seduces you to spend, spend, spend?

At the shops / in the superstore/ at home On line or watching TV shopping channel / commuting to work / in the restaurant /out in the pubs and clubs / in the bookies / in the travel agents / at the health spa / in the games shop / in the showroom / out on day trips /other ....

When my spending is at its worst I am ....
(You can also refer to you receipts)

Hey Big Spender 'get an emotional grip'

3 - Who's with you & RED?

- Who is with you when spend like you do?

Just RED and I / friends / partner / the kids / work colleagues / parents or other members of my family / other

When I spend at my worst I am with ....

4 - RED Behaviour

Your body language can tell you a secret or two. Imagine you can see yourself spending at your very worst through a pair of binoculars.

Are you; frantically searching the sale rails / excited to be shopping / saying *yes* to the kids / pressing the buy it switch on the computer or TV remote / rushing around the shops / shopping tired with my eyes practically shut / stressed making a grab for things / filling out the betting slip / propping up the bar / other

Describe your behaviour when you impulse or emotionally spend the most...........

....

....

5 - RED Money

- What do you spend your money on?

Clothes / shoes / accessories / food / chocolate / DVD's or CDs / alcohol / cars / antiques / toys / gadgets / takeaways / hobbies / home comforts / books / pampering / gifts / for the pets / lottery tickets / computer games / other ....

Ann Carver

I mainly buy ....

- How do you pay for what you buy?

Cash / credit card / debit card / someone else's money / other ....
Do you borrow money to pay for your spending? Yes/No If yes, from who? ....
How much are you capable of spending in this mode £ ....

6 - The Buzz

- What do you get out of spending money like you do *(If you didn't get anything out of it, you wouldn't do it, would you?)*

I feel confident / filling my time / I feel sexy / I get a high / I feel distracted / I feel special / powerful / generous / competitive / rich / I love being in my own little world / I feel sociable / I feel important / other ....

What do you get out of spending money in this way? ....

7 - I.D

- When I'm in a RED mood, who do I see myself to be?

Top of fashion / wining against the On Line competition / overcompensating with the kids / a control freak / the person out shopping instead of at home bored / in need of a little retail therapy / other ....

Who am I ....

Guarantee; *If you carry on doing what you've always done, nothing will change*

TIP: Feel good factor. You will never get rich by treating money poorly or feeling bad about it. Learn to treat money good then watch as it turns from RED to pearly white

Part TWO—7 Steps to Outsmart RED and find the Pearls

Now you are going to backtrack along the path you have just explored, only this time in a different frame of mine, as if you were walking in someone else's shoes, who was extremely savvy and smart with money and without RED around.

> *The only way you're going to truly change your financial life is to commit to changing the thinking patterns that got you in debt in the first place.*
> —Earl Nightingale

Mentally Preparing to Outsmart RED

The more upbeat frame of mind you can be in for the next stage of the game of outsmarting RED, the better your chances of success. Before you start, drink a glass of water and maybe sit and meditate. Now think of a fulfilling moment in your life, such as a wedding, a baby being born, or a personal achievement—any occasion that puts you in a good frame of mind. Adjust your posture and smile a big smile.

Also know that you're not alone, as there are many people like you who are breaking free from their spending habits too. Know that by telling RED to take a splash you will get your money and life back on track and end up wearing the pearls. Then complete the next steps.

TIP Throughout the exercise if you feel the presence REDs energy, STOP for a moment, take a deep breath and re-capture your new upbeat frame of mind. See your wallet / purse getting fatter and RED shrinking smaller. Most of all believe this can be done.

7 - New I.D

Imagine RED has taken a BIG splash. Now he's no longer around, see yourself physically acting smarter with money and life than ever before. Once again picture this scene as if you're looking through binoculars and zoom in. Money is now your best friend, it has the WOW factor. Also feel as you are discovering a brand-new part of you that far outweighs any material things. Describe your new identity ....

I'm enjoying my wardrobe instead of shopping for more / I'm listening my real needs / I'm being more creative and expressing my emotions in better ways / I'm a lot more patient / I'm more relaxed and having time quality out / I am myself / other ....

Describe the new you . . . I am ....

6 - The Buzz

- How are you benefiting from the new you?

I am a lot more confident / I have a new found appreciation / I feel sexier than ever/ I'm on a natural high / I feel focused / I'm empowered / truly competitive / richer / I love being in my own little world / I feel sociable / I feel valued / other ....

Describe your new buzz ....

5 - Money

- Now you're money habits have changed for the better, how are you using money instead?

RED Dot Shopping and saving at least 10% / planning and being more organized / calculating offers / setting boundaries with the family / investing wisely / paying off the debts / educating myself / cooking more home food / getting healthy / working with a life coach / setting up a business / looking for ways to increase my income/other ....

I am..

4 - New Behaviour

Imagine you can now see yourself through a pair of binoculars.

Are you; Getting from the start to the finish of the day in pocket / attending seminars and learning about money and life / sweeping 10%, 20% or even 30% of money into a savings account / talking confidently about money with the family / doing better things with my time / shopping with calm and control / taking time to think and plan my future ....

Fast-forward the brand new you to a year from now . . . describe how has your life changed ....
....

3 - Who is with me now?

My partner / kids / a mentor or coach / just me / someone new / other ....

Where's RED? ....

2 - The Place? Where are you now?

Now pinpoint the environment you are in. Perhaps you're in a new career, if so describe where, or at college or in a learning environment, maybe you're at home, perhaps you've moved somewhere different, running a business?

Describe the place ....

Describe how you are now feeling? ....

1 - New Statement

The final step requires a second signature that clarifies your commitment to continuing this process until it becomes second nature.

Your Name .... Signature .... Date ....

CREDIT to YOU

Hey Big Spender 'get an emotional grip'

23 Ways to Build Your *NO* Muscle

1. **TELL!** When pirates are caught, they are made to walk the plank. Keep telling your spending pirate to *'take a walk'* each time he tempts you to buy what you don't plan. See RED losing his grip and taking a splash!
2. **ANNOY** - Remember RED hates shopping lists, being organized, budgeting, credit cards that stay at home, and a keeping a tight ship.
3. **TAKE OWNERSHIP** - *(own your ship)*. Take hold of the helm and steer your money and life in a new direction.

4. **THINK** - Before you leave home each day, ask yourself *'what do I intend to spend'* so you kick your brain in gear at the very start. Write the amount on a Post-it Note: *Today I intend to spend £*..........................
5. **RESIST** - When temptation strikes *(as it often will at first)*, notice it pull you toward items you didn't intend to buy and then pull back. If mysterious items somehow make it to the trolley *(pirates are good at that)*, put them back!
6. **FIGHT** - The moment you step foot in a shop, imagine that you are wearing protective body armour to win the battle against RED. Drop the *'poor old me'* attitude. Instead, walk tall, smile, and tell yourself, *I'm saving a fortune.*
7. **CHECK OUT** - See how much richer you are after week one of Red Dot Shopping and aim to get richer and richer every single week.
8. **BODY SHOP** - Your body language tells yourself and other people *(such as the sales assistant, the kids, and RED)* of your spending intentions.

   55% of communication is reflected by body language.

   - Is your body language your best asset or a liability?
   - Do you walk away from tempting offers or do you walk in blind?
   - Do you always get a big trolley when a basket would do?
   - Do you look for better deals or grab the first offer you see?

9. **KNOW** that every time you physically *stop, resist,* and *walk away,* you will fatten your wallet/purse.
10. **BREATHE DEEP** to reduce anxious buying. Practice the following power breathing technique: Inhale for one breath, hold for four, exhale for two Repeat three times.
11. **WALK** - When you need just a few items, walk to the shops. *Don't call a cab to bring you back.* RED hates walking!
12. **MAKE BETTER DECISIONS** - Once you've made a decision to buy or not to buy, stick to it. If it's a bad decision, feel the pinch and improve next time.
13. **DON'T RUSH** - Relax and take your time

Hey Big Spender 'get an emotional grip'

14. **BUILD YOUR NO MUSCLE WITH THE KIDS** and have fun together in other ways. Learning to read your kids body language when out shopping will save you money and teach them good spending habits too. You can leave the kids at home, but this won't be teaching them to build their own resilience. As for temper tantrums, either ignore them or dare to model their behaviour. Feed the kids before you go shopping too. Draw your children's attention away from the items that they want by looking ahead and walking away. Be sure to relax with the kids whilst out shopping. Know that you're the one in control of your purse strings. Also sit them down and tell them you are all in a game of shopping savvy and saving as much as you can together. And don't feel you have to explain your assertiveness otherwise they will see it as weakness.

"Right, Kids lets talk about pocket money."

> *Teach your kids to shop smart at an early age, as they are easily enticed into believing that any object that is brightly coloured, noisy, messy or scorned at by parents must be cool.*
>
> — Anon

15. **SPECIAL OFFERS** can save you lots of money providing they are items that you'll definitely use *(within a few months)*.
16. **START** using cash more and plastic less.
17. **THROW** out all catalogues.
18. **SWITCH OFF** TV shopping channels and *don't* browse the Web when you're bored.
19. **EXPRESS** yourself in ways other than shopping. Get creative and energized.
20. **ASK** for professional help. If you feel out of control, you probably are.
21. **GO** easy on yourself. If you do slip up, enjoy it and don't feel bad otherwise, you'll roller coast.
22. **DON'T** pre spend your wages
23. **SHOP SMART**

7

Emotional Shopping Fix

Shopping was a way for me to soothe my moods, to put on a brave face and pretend everything was all right, when deep down it wasn't. Once in debt, this façade had the adverse effect, as I would feel guilty and ashamed with the distress that it was causing my husband, my kids, my business and myself. I would also justify my purchases and tell myself I was buying for the family, as a way of thanking them for putting up with me and my often out-of-control personality. I would buy for the business, telling myself that one day it would grow. I continued to pull the wool over people's eyes for as long as I could.

I'd spent a big part of my life hurting. Shopping was the one thing I thought couldn't hurt me. But I was so wrong. I also spent a big part of my life being frightened. I thought shopping would take away my pain and make me feel OK. *Wrong again!* But once in recovery, I got brave enough to face my fears, and the healing process dispersed the darkness. I began to see my life situation for what it was, not what I feared it might be. Frightened of facing my fears, frightened of being alone, frightened of being hurt—this is what I had to let go.

From that moment on, I got brave enough to look, to listen, and to follow my intuition. From that moment on, I would meditate, contemplate, and stand in the dark long enough to see the stars, to avoid emotional shopping and adding yet another layer to the facade. I remember the deep hurts, the deep pains, and the parts of me that I couldn't explain to family and friends or to the people I felt passionate about, for I felt that if I did, I might drive them away. No, I couldn't bear that. But ironically, in the end, I did anyway. I started shopping to put a plaster on the hurt, to disguise the pain. I could pretend all was OK and tuck this part of myself to the bottom of my soul, where it could keep quiet and hidden in the dark for a very long time, what seemed like eternity looking back now. Hiding behind something new would disguise my feelings.

In my recovery, I began to realise that this sleeping giant wasn't a sleeping monster but the essence of my being, the star in the night. Then I began to see a glimmer as I stood and took a long look and began to love and accept myself just as I am.

- **Emotionally shopping for what?**

Emotional spending is used to express pent-up emotions, to distract yourself in tough times, to hide how you truly feel, to empower yourself, to be creative, to self-heal, and to self-harm. It's the same whether you shop, socialize, gamble, or give it all away.

When life emotionally overwhelms you, sudden bursts of impatience, frustration, anger, and tears can take you by surprise . . . and in the most unexpected places. No wonder spending money and trying to buy your way out of facing pent-up emotions is chosen as an alternative way to express your feelings! How many bags can you carry? Although this antidote is a much more glamorous approach to facing your problems, it's *not* the solution—a temporary distraction, perhaps, but that's all!

- **Why doesn't it work?**

You cannot buy fulfilment, happiness, love, confidence, or security from the shop shelves. You may think that the items you continue to buy deliver or replace certain feelings, and emotional spending may work for a short while. However, it has a high price tag attached as the addiction to spendaholism kicks in. Sadly, for some people, this quick fix to feel better has become like a daily dose of medication. It's easy for you to fill your needs emotionally in the material world with new cars, designer clothes, and the many other hundreds of items you buy. And it's OK while life is running smooth and you have the money to pay. But the real challenges arise when a tragedy or a trauma strikes, such as bereavement, divorce, abuse, or job loss (to name a few), as these events can easily send you into a state of distress that leaves you feeling out of control and vulnerable.

- **Friends and family**

Friends and family may be supportive, but they have their own busy lives to lead. Also, some people you thought were your friends can reveal very different sides to their characters and turn their backs on you in times of need, because like you, they don't know how to cope either. Plus our Western culture has ingrained the belief that keeping a stiff upper lip when life gets hard is best. So the very thought of burdening other people with your problems or turning to an unknown organization or visiting the doctor seems the unglamorous option, compared to spending money and time shopping or fixing yourself through pampering and partying. The quick fix buzz of spending money to feel better, just for today—after all one day it'll be all right—wins hands down, and before you know it, you're hooked.

- **The easy option**

No matter how many material possessions you buy, it will never be enough. You'll always want more, for shopping to feel good will never satisfy your true inner needs. No doubt your bank balance, credit card statements, and possible debts already reflect your emotional spending sprees.

Two Battles

As an emotional spender, you have two battles on your hands:

1. **Internal battle:** recognising and addressing the underlying issues that originally triggered you to spend

2. **External battle:** resisting consumerism's clever marketing campaigns that are specially designed to tempt you into spending what you hadn't planned

Unpredictable

Emotions are described in the dictionary as 'strong feelings' which are often unpredictable. However, your emotions are a completely natural and healthy part of being human. Suppressed anger leads to depression and unexpressed or suppressed emotions are impossible to keep a lid on. You may think you're the one in control, but in some way or another, your spending habits will reflect a different picture. Learning to express anger and frustrations can appear to be daunting and embarrassing. Yet learning to do so in a constructive and healthy ways is a vital part of your healing process.

- When your life hits a crisis point, do you give yourself the time and space to come to terms with your situation?
- Do you search for the right type of help to meet your emotional needs?

Emotional Shopping List

Circle the following emotions that accompany you on your spending sprees ....

Love / Happiness / Hope / Enthusiasm / Gratitude / Shame / Fear / Anger / Guilt / Depression / Pride / Jealousy / Self Pity / Anxiety / Resentment / Envy / Frustration / Shame / Excitement / Denial / Regret / Sadness / Worry / Grief

1. Write down all the emotions that you experience in an average shopping week

....

2. List the day-to-day situations that trigger your desire to spend *(e.g. stress at work, pressure from kids, in company of peers):*

....

Instant Reward

Shopping to feel better gives you an instant boost. If you're down and enables you to express moods such as excitement and joy. If you could use shopping as an occasional antidote, then no real damage would be done; as it's the equivalent to having the odd glass of wine and leaving it at that. However, the trouble begins when you begin to crave more and more and take flight to the shops instead of fearlessly facing your feelings.

- **But emotional spending is harmless, isn't it?**

After all, it's not like an illegal drug or drinking too much alcohol. Besides, we've been encouraged by lenders to borrow and spend. Emotional spending should come with a health warning, as it's like any other bad habit. Relationships end in divorce, debt accumulates and people even take their own lives. Distress and living in fear of losing your worldly possessions also takes over your life. If you do look for help to deal with an emotional crisis, the immediate solutions, such as seeing doctors and attending counselling, can seem scary and unappealing and put you on even more of a downward spiral. So you can fully understand that the quick-fix buzz of emotional spending enables you to feel better just for today. Thousands of men and women do this every day as a way of putting on braver faces. After all, one day it'll be all right. Plus it makes perfect sense to buy something new to boost your mood rather than take your misery out on someone else or have to spend time addressing the root cause, doesn't it?

The following is a sad story of lady who lived in Guernsey. Both her husband and her son died from motorcycle accidents. Over a decade later she was found dead on the beach. She had suffered a heart attack whilst walking her dog. When her friend went to help clear the house where she had lived, she was astounded to find many of unopened boxes and clothes with the labels still on. She had turned to shopping to distract her from her sadness, as a result she accumulated huge debt and was losing her house, the stress had become unbearable for her.

- Has shopping become your outlet to express your overwhelming emotions?
- Have you noticed that it's doing you more harm than good as of late?

Change for the better

With the right help, you can change your destructive spending habits for better ones and discover a unique part of you that is waiting to be found and treasured from the inside out, *not* the outside in! Overwhelming emotions that trigger you to spend only seem to be acknowledged when you finally begin to feel the consequences of your spending habits. So learning to put yourself in a healthy emotional state and coming to terms with underlying issues that are bugging you are crucial, as the better you feel about your life, the more respect you'll give to yourself and your money.

You can change your emotional spending habits for better by doing the following:

1. Recognising the emotions that trigger you to spend
2. Taking ownership and admitting that it's time for change
3. Giving love and time to yourself
4. Learning to express your emotions in healthy ways that will not cost you
5. Educating yourself on how money and life work
6. Getting the right help to deal with your situation

Power Questions

- What major events have happened in your life that you use shopping to disguise?
- What do you get out of shopping and spending money?
- What's it costing you?
- Why do you want to stop spending like you do?
- What would happen if you didn't stop?
- What would happen if you did?

> *You cannot control or predict the storms in life, but you can determine the way you set the sail.*
> —Jim Rohan

Note: If addiction to alcohol or drugs is an issue for you, then I strongly recommend you seek to tackle this problem. There are organizations listed at the back of this book to assist you.

Dropping the Emotional Shopping Baggage

- How much longer can you afford to keep up your emotional shopping sprees?

It's time to stop stuffing your unaddressed emotions in bags and taking them home. But before you take the first step, I want you to understand a bit more about it. As an emotional shopper, there's no doubt you're got used to buying your way out of your painful life experiences. And as you well know, this way of dealing with things comes at a price. Now emotional spending has a grip on you, leaving you a double whammy to face.

1. You have an emotional shopping habit to kick
2. You have to be brave and face the underlying issues that triggered you to shop in the first place.

When you originally began to emotionally shop, it seemed the more glamorous option to overcome your personal adversities, but I'm sure you now know that all that glitters is not gold!

When the going gets tough, the tough get going!

When you're going through a tough time, often people close to you try to soothe your situation by telling you not to feel angry or not to worry about it, mainly because, like you, they don't know what to do or say either. Even when you turn to professional help, it doesn't guarantee to help you in the way that is best for you. So Instead of being listened to and allowed to constructively express your feelings, you suppress them and act in ways that are more secretive, disguised amongst the material world, and your hurts get covered up instead of healed. Within a few years, you accumulate hoards of possessions which reflect your unexpressed emotional baggage. Your suppressed emotions leads to depression, which you use spending money to bridge, but it fails to get to the root cause of your problems. If only we could buy our way out. Yes, emotional spending it provides a temporary release, but that's it—until the next time.

Wealth Sabotage

Each time you go shopping to defuse depression and anger, you will sabotage wealth, as this way of coping with your feelings will keep you in debt on an emotional level; not dealing with your crisis in a constructive way, will leave you in debt to your feelings. Additionally, this reflects on a financial level, for your suppressed emotions triggers you to uncontrollably shop and spend money you don't intend to. Keith Tondour, author of *Your Money Your Life*, states, 'A person's financial crisis is a reflection of their emotional, mental, and spiritual life'.

Power of Emotion

Emotions are designed to move you through situations; they power you through in the same way a ship rides the waves of a storm, by facing it. Unfortunately, lack of education, especially in the Western world, as to knowing how to deal with such powerful feelings creates fear in individuals. This makes dealing with such strong feelings overwhelming and so people chose turn away as the easier option, or so they think. Many people don't know which way to turn when life gets emotionally challenging, and they become vulnerable as they try to deal with their situation in the best way they can. Sadly, for many people, this means drinking alcohol, taking drugs, going shopping, being put on unnecessary pharmaceutical medication, and falling prey to companies that charge big interest fees! These methods of dealing with emotional issues are powerfully destructive, as they lead to ill health, debt, and dependency.

Linda described her debt as a *'heavy stone she was carrying around in her head'*.

If people were educated to face their fears in ways that were constructive and creative, such as through art, dance, talking and being listened to, meditation, and getting the right support, then as a nation, we would be a happier and less dependent, with a lot less ill health and debt. Yet it's almost alien be gentle and kind towards yourself in times such as loss, especially with modern demands and limited time to go through a natural healing process. As a result, your life centres around making yourself feel better by shopping etc. Perhaps you go shopping to avoid spending time alone after a loss, or to de-stress from a hectic time at work, or as a way to make up for family time out. Whatever your excuse, it's time to delve deeper and find a new vice, one that is a lot less expensive and more satisfying.

Remember that depression and anger are not to be messed with, suppressed, or ignored, as they're too big for you to contain. Ill health and disease such as depression, high blood pressure, cancer, nervous breakdowns, and debt, to name a few, can be caused by unexpressed feelings. The next four steps are designed to help you recognise and drop your emotional baggage. By the end of the process, I hope you will begin to feel unburdened, happier, and a lot less harsh on your wallet and purse.

6 Steps to STOP Carrying Emotional Baggage Around

1st Step—Visualization Feel the Weight

Imagine that you have two strong, empty carrier bags. Go to the beach and fill the bags with pebbles; the pebbles represent your pent-up feelings. When the bags are full, walk along the beach. As you walk, feel the weight of the bags get heavier and heavier. Your arms ache, and your neck and back feel the strain; your knees want to give way. The bags are almost too heavy to carry. When you can't go any further, push yourself to walk some more. Similar your body and mind a feel the strain of the emotional baggage you have been carrying around, only they can do you a lot more harm than when you try to physically carry the heavy bags. Know that you have two choices;

1. You can continue to carry your problems around with you and to emotionally spend each time life gets too much
2. Or you can choose to drop your emotional baggage, walk free, and be liberated.

2nd Step—What's Missing

It is important to identify what you are using retail therapy and spending money to replace. When you fail to pinpoint what is missing from your life, you will grasp at straws trying to make yourself feel better. When a relationship breaks down, you may hear a person say that 'they have a split from their partner', but very rarely will the person describe the love that was lost. When a person loses a job or their home is repossessed they say' they have lost their job or their home', but they do not speak about the loss of security.

It In order for healing to take place, it is important to identify what was taken from you in times of change, be it love, security, companionship, peace, and so forth, and then look to replace the lost feelings in ways that will heal you and not cause you anymore harm.

When I began shopping to feel better, I was really looking for the love that had been lost. Looking back now no material thing could ever replace what had gone. When I look back now the loved ones are gone, but the love is still there, and I can express this is many other ways than shopping.

- Maybe you've suffered a loss and feel your love has gone
- Perhaps you've experienced abuse and feel as though your confidence and dignity has gone
- Or have you lost a job and feel as though your security has gone

3rd Step—Identifying the Missing Feelings

It's time to identify what feelings were taken from you and the person/people who were involved. When someone dies this can be challenging, as nothing or no one can replace the loss, however you can work to gradually re-store the feelings that went.

Examples

- I identify that when my mother passed my love and relationship with her were physically missing and I used to shop to try and replace these.
- I identify that when my marriage to Jonathon broke down my love and security went and I used to shop for comfort
- Can you identify a life crisis where precious feelings were taken from you?
- What were the feelings and who was the person/people involved?

4th Step—Dropping the Baggage

Now that you recognise what was missing, the next step is to drop the emotional baggage. So you release any unhealthy emotional ties that may be costing you big time and walk free. Know the only debt you owe is to love and accept your situation and yourself for what it is, nothing else matters, so the situation and the people involved are free and so are you.

Commitment Statement

I now choose to replace what is missing by loving and accepting the situation for what it is

Signed...

Repeat this process for all debts and all of your life hurts that you recognise you have been holding onto for far too long.

5th Step—To Forgive and Forget

People often struggle with the act of forgiveness, as they feel they have to approach the person concerned which can appear threatening or make defences go up, but this is not so. First and foremost forgiveness is a feeling or a vibe you give out, it is heartfelt, it is not something you have to physically carry out. You can use the power of forgiveness to free yourself and others of past hurt, which enable you to let go of emotional baggage and stop carrying unnecessary pent up emotions around. Whether you feel a person owes you an explanation or an apology or you owe them one, the higher ground is to forgive and let go.

Forgiving doesn't mean you forget, as your memory can act as a protection mechanism, to stop you from repeating the harmful process all over again. However, you can also keep opening up old wounds, if you chose to churn over the past and never give the situation time to heal. If you had a broken leg you wouldn't

Hey Big Spender 'get an emotional grip'

continue to walk on it would you? No you would give it time to heal, but the next time you were on the same ski slope that you broke it on, you would act with caution. However people usually deal with hurt in two ways that do not work.

1. They imagine they're back in the situation. This connects them with the past memories and the feelings they experienced at the time come flooding back. And then the guards go up.
2. They try their hardest to ignore or control the powerful feeling and in the process suppress them, which in turn leads to depression and a build up of resentment.

Know that choosing to harbour unforgiveness eats away at you in the form of bitterness and the damning affects will definitely do you more harm than good. So just to clarify, you <u>do not</u> have to tell or involve the person concerned, and it is best not to as they may not be accepting and push your forgiveness away and trample over the whole process. Know the feeling of release for you is of utmost importance. So learn to follow through the process and feel the benefits for your sake more than anything. Know that *you are the change* and forgiveness liberates you first and foremost and quite rightly so.

6th Step—Focus Future

No doubt you will still experience overwhelming feelings from time to time, as they come in waves. Life is never plain sailing, especially if you are under the weather or your hormones are playing you up or you are going through a particular sensitive time, but that doesn't mean you have to buy into such feelings. Imagine a ship sailing on a turbulent waters, the captain will not let the ship sink, but he will centre himself at the helm and hold firm and steady until he has out ridden the waves. Each time you are reminded of past unpleasant situations, remember you are free and ride the temporary storm out. As the storm passes, your feelings will lighten and your low mood will gradually uplift without much harm done. Nothing happens overnight so learn to be patient. Make a daily decision to keep history in its place and tell yourself it's the future that counts. This is where meditation will also help, so if you can sit with your feelings, count your breaths and let whatever it is pass. And most of all don't go shopping!!

I was reading an article about a man with a little boat who saw a tsunami approaching. He took his boat and walked towards it, facing it head-on, and miraculously he made it through.

Treasure *You* Time

Taking time out to relax is an absolute tonic for you. This following relaxation takes you through a process that enables you to let go of tension, in your body and mind, know you will get out what you put in. If you can ask someone to read this out to you first time round.

Relaxation: Coming to Your Senses

It's time for you to treasure yourself over beyond anyone or anything. I want you to know that you are worth every ounce of effort you are putting in. From now on, you're number one on the list to love and get to know. Whilst out shopping, your senses are sent wild, and you are enticed and teased to the extreme. This following relaxation will help you to come to your senses and find a new you to treasure from the inside out . . . and the best thing of all is that it doesn't cost a dime, only 10-15 minutes of your time, daily if you can.

Instructions

1. Lay with support for your head, making sure you're warm enough, and close your eyes. Allow the floor beneath to take the complete weight of your body.

Hey Big Spender 'get an emotional grip'

2. Your senses are made up of touch, taste, sight, sound, and smell. Take your attention to your feet and toes and relax them. Relax your legs and relax your trunk. Drop the weight of your shoulders towards the ground and away from your neck. Relax your arms, your hands and your fingers, and your sense of touch. Feel that your head is centred and smooth out any tensed creases over your forehead and around your eyes. Close your eyelids, relaxing your sense of sight, and get a glimpse of a new you that you're beginning to treasure. Take your attention to your mouth and your sense of taste, knowing that you're getting a taste of what is good for you. Relax your tongue on your lower palate and relax and unclench your jaws. Take your attention to your ears and imagine they have a volume control that is being adjusted to quiet mode. Listen to your breath.
3. Breathe through your nose and soften your nostrils so they do not harshly inflate. As you inhale, your nostrils stay soft; as you exhale, begin to let go from the inside out. Know that for these precious moments, there's no need to hold on. Simply let go of any control and just be. As you inhale, imagine that you're breathing in towards a golden nougat of treasure that sits within you . . . As you exhale, sense a warm glow that is flowing throughout. Feel it release it throughout the whole of your being. Stay relaxed for 10 minutes.
4. Now it's time to release from your relaxation, but know that you can return to this new part of you tomorrow and the next. Know that taking time to relax is absolutely priceless for you. Feel the firmness of the floor beneath you, take a deep breath and gradually open your eyes. What a little gem you are for giving yourself this time. Just before you get up, smile to yourself. I recommend that you return to this relaxation daily. As you release from relaxation, read these following quotes:

*Abundance is not something we acquire; it's something
we tune into.*
—Wayne Dyer

Victory belongs to the most persevering.
—Napoleon

If you don't take the time to look, you simply react.
—Dr. John F. Demartini

*There are always gifts in failures,
if you dare to unwrap them.*
—Ann Carver

Face up to what you fear, and fear is removed.
—Anonymous

*Instead of yearning, desiring and waiting for money
spend some time every day learning about your inner
relationship with money. Prosperity starts in the mind.*
—Cappi Pidwell

You're worthy and worth all the effort you're putting in.
—Ann Carver

From the Inside Out

You cannot see love, but you can feel it, whether it's your heart beating or breaking. You cannot see forgiveness, but you can feel the release when you practice it. You cannot see freedom, but you can breathe it. Know that there is a higher force at work on your behalf, if you chose to tune in to it. Believe that there is a universal source capable of reversing your lot. As you do, doors of opportunity open for you, as like attracts like.

Meditation

Create a small space in your home in which to meditate and retreat to every day. Put a symbol to represent money and abundance flowing into your life and a candle. Meditate at the same time daily if you can, preferably in the morning or evening. Notice as your life begins to run more smoothly. Think of meditation as a way of showing gratitude towards yourself for the effort you are putting into your life. Begin with just 5 minutes a day. Just sit and count your breaths from 1-10, repeat 3 times. There is nothing to fear—only inner peace and love to be found.

Inhale abundance into your life and exhale all tension that has built up in your mind and body. Imagine that you are a money magnet and the tide is turning in your direction. Learn to accept that money is coming your way.

Walking

Just put on your shoes and step out of the door. Fresh air and exercise leave you feeling great and doesn't cost a penny. Where can you walk to where you would normally drive? Learn to recapture a sense of appreciation for your local area on the journey.

I believe there is a universal energy that is bigger than anyone can comprehend. All it asks of you is to embrace it. If you want to experience this to its full potential, learn to accept the wonder of it all. Daily *wow* moments are there for you in the most beautiful and simplistic ways. Know that life wants you as much as you want it. Know that you are loved. Learn to love life, and above all yourself, in as many ways you can. Whether you sit and appreciate, contemplate, meditate, or create, take time to look and believe that there are gems if you are willing to look.

8

Vision & Goals

Imagine a picture on the wall of what you want your future to look like—then desire it with all your heart and make it happen.

This section is designed for you to create an ideal picture of what you want in your future and then set the necessary goals to make it happen. A vision is a powerful tool that will focus your attention and enable you to achieve in life. RED hates it when you begin to look to the future with more precision, as he knows it'll be a lot harder to entice you to overspend. Yet life without a vision enables RED to jump on board easily and rob your future. Creating a picture in your mind of where you desire to be is also the golden key to avoid being emotionally overwhelmed in recovery, as it keeps your head above the water and moving towards the solution. And because your vision is a lot rosier than your present affairs, this builds momentum for you to work on it step by step. Once you make a start it won't be long before you are looking back and realising how far you have come. And as for RED he will be long gone.

- Just imagine your future, if you accept your situation for what it is and carry on hitting the spending switch

- Now imagine you are reaping the rewards from the vision you created

When I met Vicky, she had hit a financial crisis and didn't know which way to turn. She felt confused and unhappy. She said she did not know what she wanted anymore. I asked her if she could remember a moment in her life when her dreams had come true. After shedding some tears, she looked up with a glint in her eye and suddenly remembered the powerful moment of wanting to live in England as a child.

'When I was a child in China, I used to dream of living in England. Every day I would go into the rice fields, and each time I saw a plane in the sky, I would imagine being on the plane, flying to England. My grandmother used to tell me to believe in my dreams. Now I live in England.'

Vicky knew that the key to life was to have a dream and follow it, but once she'd achieved this she lost sight and became complacent, but once she recognised this she knew she could tap into her inner resources and use her skills to fulfil other dreams.

Imagine

A captain of a ship set sails to Australia. When he sets off, he can't see the land he is heading towards and won't do until he practically reaches it. But until then all he can do is see it on the map, imagine it in his mind and plan the journey. Imagine if he set sail without a destination to head for . . . . he would have no purpose for setting sail, plus he could end up anywhere. He could find paradise, if lady luck was with him, but equally he could sail into shark-infested waters or be captured by pirates. The captain of the ship will not gamble with his chances of success, but will navigate and use his head.

Leadership equals leading your ship.

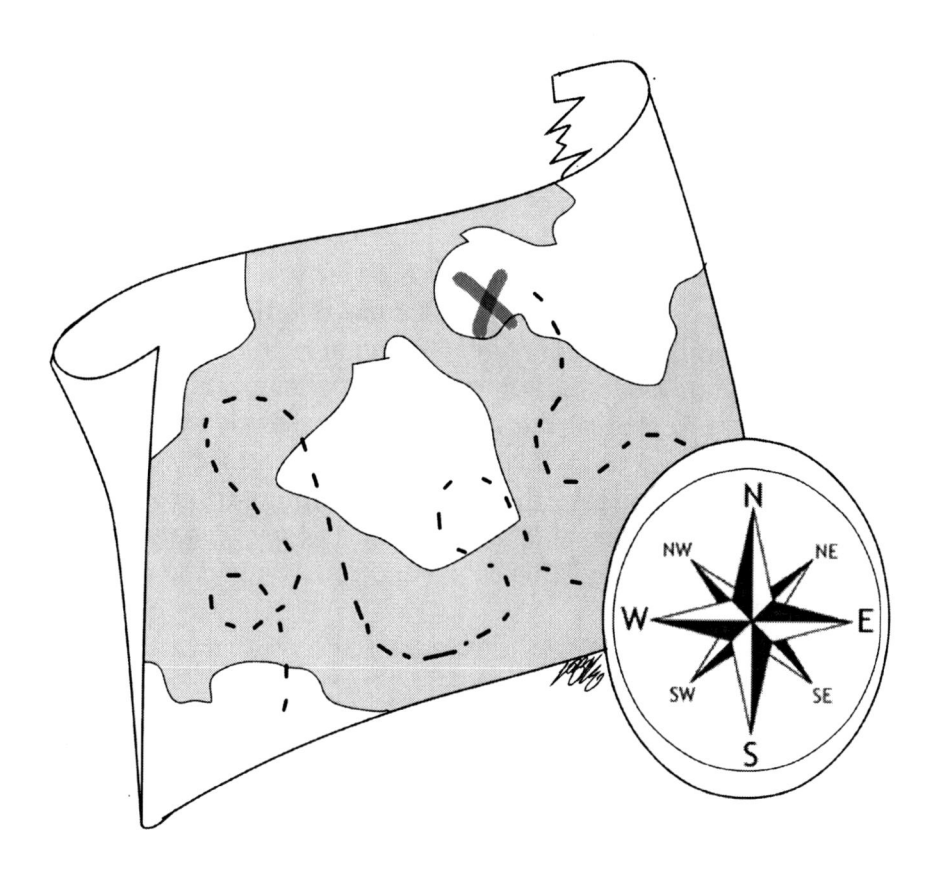

With or without a Vision

Visions are future orientated. A vision stretches your thinking from the short-term buzz that quickly fades, towards creating a much more satisfying future. Impulse and emotional spending paints a bleak and uncertain picture of your future. Yet setting a vision and creating a plan for you and your money is what makes dreams real. The purpose of having dreams is to turn them into reality isn't it? Yes, there will be storms to ride along the way and lessons to learn, but you will get there if you keep persisting and believing you can.

- Can you remember a time when you desired to achieve an ambition?

Maybe this was for a wedding, a holiday, or to one day fall in love. Do you recall the elements of apprehension and excitement in the process of playing the waiting game? How about the sense of appreciation when you finally received what you were longing for? And the afterthought of knowing you could achieve anything if you put your mind to it.

Yet life without a vision makes it easy for you to be distracted or, even worse, stay in uncomfortable life situations. If you have no vision or ambition, your life can carry on in the same habitual patterns for your entire life. But know your money and life can easily change course by seeing your situation as you ideally want it to be and planning to set to sail. Instead of being constantly worrying about the future, you take the helm and recapture control. With a vision, one day you'll be able to look back and say, 'I've ridden the storm and come out the other side'—and you'll be so glad you did!

You are 100% worth it.

Rich Vision

Wealthy people have a vision for their money and life because sustaining wealth is a top priority to them. They look to the future with financial intelligence. That's how they get rich and stay that way, *not* by spending all their money and regretting it later.

Setting a vision has been the most powerful part of my debt freedom journey. When I was in debt, I would constantly worry, as I couldn't see a way out. I was bogged down with a poverty state of mind and not going anywhere. It was as if I was drowning in despair. Then, like a crazy lady, I would go out and spend money to cheer myself up! When money ran out, I'd get another credit card or loan to clear my debts, but all I did was accumulate more and sink deeper into overwhelm.

Opening Doors

One amazing thing I've learnt about the power of a desire is that the moment I truly wanted to look for new ways forwards, life revealed new paths for me to explore. I became aware of signposts and doors of opportunities that before, when I was walking around with my eyes shut, I never saw.

Your Vision

Cast any limitations of the mind aside and ask yourself 'what do I want'. There's no doubt that one of the main reasons you've been financially and emotionally stretched to your limits is because you didn't set out with a specific plan or vision for your money or life. Setting a money vision will steer you in the right direction and enable you to get your head above any overwhelming feelings that you may be experiencing right now as you to focus on the solution, not your problem. A vision will give you the power to overcome any obstacles that get in your way, because once you discover what you truly want and start to believe that it's achievable, nothing will stand in your way. Your vision also gets you excited about life once again. Upon reaching your vision, it feels as if a long-awaited dream has come true.

> If you have built castles in the air, your work need not be lost; that is where they should be. Now put the foundations under them.
> —Henry David Thoreau

RED Warning

When you set a vision for the first time, be prepared to get uncomfortable, as you have been in your established habits a long time. In order to make positive changes, you need to get used to feeling different. You will be the same person; however, you will get better and better at being who you are. I'm sure you'll be pleasantly surprised too. Know that ships only learn to really sail in choppy waters, so don't expect your journey to be plain sailing, because it's not. Expect resistance from people around you who would prefer that you stay exactly as you are, this can sometimes come as surprise or a shock as the people you think are by your side are actually not. Other resistance is from that part of you (RED behaviour) that want to carry on being reckless. However, know that this conflict is a natural part of the process of change and once you push through it will be like you have given birth to new life!

Top Secret

In order to limit the opposition know the fewer people you tell about your vision, especially in the early days, the better. I recommend keeping your vision secret from anyone who will trample over it. If you must tell someone, then be selective and only tell those who will believe in you, encourage you, and help you to grow. I recommend getting yourself a life coach or a mentor, someone who will not judge you or tell you what to do but who will instead help you to move from where you are now to where you want to be. It's also important for your vision to be your dream and not anyone else's. Although people often do have the best intentions and attempt to give you their advice, know that this is coming from their perspective and not yours. So having non-judgemental people around you who will encourage you to grow is crucial.

Creating Your Vision

1. **Prepare** - You will need a big sheet of paper, coloured pens, and plenty of time (allow yourself at least an hour). Make certain that you won't be interrupted. Switch off the telephone and retreat to a place of quiet.

2. **Mind** - Put yourself in a good state of mind, if possible exercise or meditate before you start. The more upbeat mood you're in, the more motivated and creative you'll be. Personally, before I start, I take my dog for a refreshing walk along the beach. As I walk, I picture my future.
3. **Define your vision** - Be specific and clear. My vision is financial freedom. Look at the examples below and then think about what it is that you want for your money and life. Or look at a problem you have right now and picture the exact opposite. If you're in debt, then your vision may be financial freedom. If you are broke then perhaps wealthy is for you.

Examples

- Financially Freedom
- House Owner
- Business Owner

- What is your vision? ....

4. **Question** why you want this particular vision to come true, so you can get an idea of what this will look like and mean for your life. Spend the next five minutes writing non-stop about your vision. Go into as much description as you possibly can E.g. I want financial freedom to secure the future for myself and my family and to also write my books and develop my business. This will enable me to make a significant change for good and to live a fulfilled life etc

- Why do you want this? ....

5. **Figure** - How much money will you need. If you're in debt, calculate how much you owe. If you want to start a business, then decide how much you need to start. If you want to be financially secure then work out how much you will need for this, put a figure on it. If you have no idea then research and find out. Write this figure down.

6. **Route** - Decide the route you're going to take to reach your vision. Maybe you want to educate yourself on how money really works or get reputable debt help. Perhaps you want to decide on a new a new career or take a business course? *I wanted to be financially free and knew my behaviour that had got me in debt had to change. So the route I chose was life coaching and NLP*
7. **Momentum** - Take action every single day that drives you in the direction of your vision. *Bring it to life.*

- Today I'm going to ....

- Tomorrow I'm going to ....

- The next day I'm going to..

- And the next week I'm going to..

The Magic Key

Each and every day think of your vision, even if you are unsure of the next steps to take I urge you to picture it. If you feel overwhelmed with debt or a current life crisis and this seems an impossible task, it's important to trust the process and set your sights high. Make your vision a lot bigger and brighter that your present reality. The universe is like a giant magnet, attracting like with like, so think big and feel the universal pull as you are drawn towards the vision that you set. Notice opportunities present them self to you and act upon them. Prepare to be surprised, for often visions come to fruition a lot faster than you can comprehend.

Note

The key ingredients for your vision are belief, motivation, confidence, desire, passion, and the faith to believe that what you see in your mind will one day happen. These key treasures don't cost a dime—just an investment in your time that pays off in more ways that you can ever imagine!

Bon voyage!

9

For 'Richer or Poorer'

Listed below is a mix of beliefs about money. Read the list and highlight the beliefs that ring true with you.

Having money is a matter of personal choice.
Money's a struggle; it's always spoken for.
Everything I want is here for when I'm ready to collect it.
Money goes to money.
Money makes the world go round.
I love money, and money loves me.
Once it's gone, it's gone.
Money doesn't make you happy.
Having money means I can impact the world around me.
I'd lose my friends if I had money.
Every penny I spend returns to me multiplied.
Great things can be done with money.
I don't owe anyone or own anything.
I can easily receive money.
Money's the root of all evil.
To have money, you have to win it, inherit it, or marry into it.
You can't take it with you.
I don't deserve to have money.
I can't be spiritual and have money.
If I were meant to have money, I would have it by now.

Money Beliefs

- What do you believe about money?

Money beliefs pass through generations of families and can be an asset or a liability, a blessing or a curse, depending if they were good or bad and how you perceived them to be. Your beliefs about money will determine whether money will work for you or against you, and they will reflect how you and your money tick. If you were bought up in a family that managed money well, then these good lessons will be a natural part of your make-up, unless you decide to believe otherwise! If you were bought up in a family that had limited skills and feared there was never enough, then this can limit your knowledge as an adult, unless you choose to learn the necessary skills that you need to manage on a new level of intelligence.

- The word *belief* equals a principle or idea accepted as true, especially without proof.
- The word *liability* equals someone or something that causes a problem.

Beliefs that are liabilities cause you unnecessary worry and fears, also blocking financial progress. However, you can change your destiny by installing new beliefs, which in turn will help you manage money with profound confidence. Practicing better beliefs can allow miracles to happen and transform your life from rags to riches.

> It is preoccupation with possessions, more than anything else, that prevents us from living freely and nobly. —Bertrand Russell

Example 1: If you believe there's no way out of your financial situation, you'll feel worried and unable to think straight, forever feeling wrapped up in the anxiety of it all. As a result, you'll continue to make matters worse, like being caught on a hamster wheel, so believing there's no way out will keep you trapped in this limited mindset.

Example 2: If you believe you'll become financially free, you'll begin to feel more confident and set your sights towards a brighter future. As a result, your eyes will be open to windows of opportunity, for you will attract like with like and take the necessary action to evoke change.

Where do beliefs come from?

As a forty-year-old woman, I never really knew what I believed about money! But as I began to find out, I realised that many of my limiting beliefs had stemmed from my family and working-class upbringing. As an adult these beliefs sat at the root of my money problems. As I began to change what I believed about money, which stemmed from learning about how it works, my beliefs changed for the better.

The beliefs that you hold about money have been stored in your subconscious mind from an early age. These come from parents, grandparents, teachers, religious and spiritual influences, the media, and anyone else who may have influenced you practically since birth. These beliefs form a big part of how you think and behave around money today. Because this process started the moment you were born, you will not identify with most of them, but your behavioural patterns with money will reflect them, depending on what you learnt or took on board. Unless you were born into a wealthy family or your parents had good morals around money, then your money beliefs will no doubt be limited, for good financial education is limited in schools and in society. Consumerism especially wants you to believe that it's good to spend, spend, spend, and that the answer to your new sofa is to get one on credit. Many people think that the answer to their prayers is to simply go and borrow. Consumerism is designed to extract your money from your wallet/purse to theirs!

Subconscious

Your subconscious mind is like a computer. A computer is not interested in what's true or false; it just operates in the way it has been programmed, by whoever has access to it. It's up to the owner to defrag and delete the unwanted files that cause it to crash. Your subconscious mind (or 'neck-top computer', as Peter Thompson calls it), needs sorting and reprogramming to work more effectively, especially where your money is concerned. As you change what you believe about money, you'll soon run more efficiently.

Role Models

Finding role models who believe in greatness and have found the determination to make something of their own lives is a great way to learn. I always feel inspired by people who have succeeded after overcoming personal obstacles. This may be a family member you admire or a friend who is wealthy. Or it may come from studying people by reading biographies such as those about Levi Roots, Alan Sugar, or Arnold Schwarzenegger—whoever inspires you. The information you learn will feed into your subconscious mind, provoke your thoughts, and in time will impact your belief system.

You will soon recognise what feelings and thoughts are worth keeping and which ones no longer serve you. The best way to find out about yourself is to get to know what you believe, because most (I'm not saying *all*) of your messy financial situations were created by your own ragged belief system.

On a positive note, nothing is wasted, and it's never too late to rewind, delete, renew, and fast-forward your life to a brand-new moment in time. And you do this by first recognising the poor beliefs that limit you. Then you work to delete and re-programme them into new beliefs that will enable you to break through the financial barriers that made you initially crash. Then you can drive your life forwards in a new direction.

Belief Shift

To help myself get to grips with life, I attended Tony Robbins's motivational seminar 'Unleash the Power Within', which I highly recommend, it is held at the Excel in London in the UK. As a metaphor for overcoming fear, Tony motivates you to walk across hot coals. The following day he gets you to face every single emotion from passion to anger in order to let the unnecessary baggage go, somehow walking on the hot coals felt easier! A big part of me wanted to resist, as I was petrified I would burn my feet or fall flat on my face. On the build-up to walking across the coals, every pathetic excuse of why I shouldn't do it showed its face. Although I was fully aware that fear is designed to protect me, I couldn't use this excuse, as walking on hot coals had been tried and tested by millions of people. As I battled with my mind, I suddenly heard a voice inside me say, *you will be like Cinderella if you do or stay as you are if you don't!* This internal voice was enough to fire me up and get me across the hot coals. My new mindset would soon prove to me within an hour that I could face extraordinary tasks.

Prior to the seminar, I discovered that I had booked the hotel on the opposite side of the Thames. This meant that I had to drive to my hotel late at night with no satnav; all I had was a map. The 'I can do anything' frame of mind I was in enabled me to get from the Excel Centre in London to my hotel without getting lost or panicking. I believed I would find it, put my mind to it, and to my amazement I did. That night I felt so elated and inspired that even Big Ben looked small as I drove past!

Instinctively, I now knew that I could get on top of life too. Why? Because I believed I could—and I wanted to more than anything else in the world!

Transformation

Let's turn the clock back to the story of Cinderella. Before her life was transformed, everyone mocked her and called her names (apart from her true friends, the mice). The only power she held over her situation was to believe that one day life would be different. Then suddenly and almost overnight, her life transformed beyond all she had ever dreamed of. OK, there was a prince involved, but you get the gist, right? Cinderella believed and emotionally desired her life to be different and she kept heart despite her hardship.

Many people pin their modern-day hopes and dreams on one day winning the lottery so they too can transform from rags to riches. But the journey of becoming rich starts from within your belief system. The trouble is that we spend so much time chasing the dream in the material world that we bury our true inner treasures, often beneath mountains of debt. This is the point when we begin to wake up and discover that the dream we were chasing was really a nightmare!

I'm talking from experience, as this happened to me. I was so caught up in the 'spend and mend Ann' syndrome that I didn't stop until I almost lost the family home. Why? Because I was programmed with a poor belief system when it came to money and also didn't believe I was worthy of a better life, so as all I ever strove for was just enough to get by on.

At the seminar, the time I spent rewinding and deleting these thoughts enabled me to fast-forward to a moment in time where I had become debt-free and enriched with wealthier beliefs. Installing new thoughts and beliefs can lead you to unlimited realms within your life. Your world really is your oyster.

'Nobody's perfect' are words I hear often. However, I chose to believe that we are *'all perfect in our own way'*. Then we can learn to accept ourselves instead of continuing to strive for perfection. We all have valuable assets about our personalities. Be it in our hearts, our minds, our bodies, our sons and daughters, our partners, our creativity, or in our smiles, the list is endless.

- What valuable assets do you have as a person?

Hey Big Spender 'get an emotional grip'

- What gifts have you been blessed with—and where are they now?

> *Spending is quick; earning is slow.*
> —Old Russian saying

> *Money is an emotional instrument, but emotions can get in the way of making the right investment decisions... If we can fathom our individual emotional tendencies, then we can take steps and correct them.*
> —Hannah Grove, Merrill Lynch Investments

Change your mind; change your money.

10

Money Memories

Katie

Looking good and buying the latest fashion were top priorities for Katie and her young daughter. As a result, she often had no money left to buy food and essentials. As she explored her money memories, sudden realization hit home. Katie had grown up in an affluent area, although her parents were not as wealthy as other families in the neighbourhood. Katie regularly played at her rich friend's house; however, whenever she needed to use the bathroom, she was made to go home by the parents.

As a woman, Katie believed she needed to look good, for deep down she was worried about what other people thought of her. This related back to her childhood experience. Money memories enabled Katie to retrace the initial root of her destructive spending patterns that she'd forgotten about in adulthood. As a result, Katie's life was transformed. She began to dress to suit herself, and she looked more natural and had a relaxed look about her. Also, for the first time, she had money left at the end of each week, which she spent having quality time out with her daughter. She also had newfound happiness and confidence and a vision to start her own business.

My 1ˢᵗ Pocket Money Memory

As a young girl, the most exciting part of my week was walking to the sweet shop with my pocket money on a Saturday morning and joining the other kids in the queue. Chocolate tools, flying saucers, sugar mice, sherbet dips, and penny sweets were kept on the counter at eye level. The back wall displayed endless jars of rosy apples, bonbons, and sugar candy, which were sold in two and four ounce bags. I remember counting how many sweets I could get for my money, and I enjoyed taking my time choosing. My first feelings and thoughts of spending money were happy.

- What are your early childhood memories with money?

My 1ˢᵗ Shopping Memory

My parents argued a lot, except on Thursday evenings, when they went shopping. Out in public, they would be on their best behaviour. I was allowed to choose treats on each shopping trip, so my shopping experience as a child was happy for me.

- What was your 1ˢᵗ shopping memory?

My 1ˢᵗ Saving Memory

My first attempt at saving was with the sweets. Each week I would save a portion of them in my bedroom draw. I built up quite a collection. However, unbeknown to me, my older brother knew. One day I returned home from school to find empty sweet wrappers littered all over my bedroom floor. He had invited his friend round, and the two of them ate them all! I felt angry that he had invaded my bedroom and stolen my sweets.

- What was your 1ˢᵗ memory of saving?

My 1st Guilty Memory

My most guilty memory growing up was when my mother had saved hard to buy me a new school coat. Up until then, I'd worn my brother's hand-me-down duffle coat. When there was enough money, we made a special trip to C & A in Reading. As soon as I arrived home from the shopping trip, I couldn't wait to wear my new coat and show it off to my mates. We went for a walk in the woods and played on the rope swing. I took my coat off and hung it on a tree so as not to ruin it. We played for a couple of hours and then headed home. And I forgot to put my coat back on; I left it hanging on the tree! As I stepped in the back door of the house, my mum looked at me with a puzzled expression on her face. 'Where's your new coat?' she enquired.

I felt my rosy cheeks drain of colour. I immediately turned and ran back to the rope swing as fast as my legs would carry me. However, my new coat was nowhere to be seen! I felt so guilty that I'd lost it on the very first day I got it, especially knowing how hard my mother had saved to buy it.

- Do you remember feeling bad about money as a child?

The 1st Time I Asked for Money

My older brother David was ten years older than I was and had a reputation for being tight with his money. One day the ice cream bell rang. An ice cream cost 5p, and I only had 4p. Then David walked by. I called out excitedly, asking him for the other penny. 'NO' he sternly replied, I knew he meant it. I remember feeling hurt at how mean he acted.

- What do you remember about your brothers or sisters money traits?

My Parents and Money

My dad lived for the moment; he didn't cope with too much with financial responsibility. After a hard week's work, he handed over the housekeeping to my mother and spent what was left down the pub. In later years, as he watched me financially struggle, he sat me down with a tear in his eye and said, 'I only wish that I had got my life together so that I could have made your journey easier!' With a gulp in my throat, I hugged him. When he passed away, he had very few belongings. On the other hand, my mother was careful and organized with her share of the money. Her motto was 'I don't own anything or owe anyone'. All the bills were paid on time.

- How were your parents with money when you were growing up?

My 1st Wage

When I was fourteen, my parents divorced. Up until then, I'd received a generous allowance for pocket money and clothes. But now that my dad wasn't around, money was scarce, so any money I wanted, I had to earn. This seemed a harsh lesson at the time, as my best friend, Shirley, was spoilt rotten by her parents. But I set to work and held down three part-time jobs in between school. My daily routine began with a paper round, from which I earned £3 a week. I would then cycle five miles to Shirley's house, where I would clean her mum's house before going to school. This earned me another £3 a week. Shirley was paid to clean as well, but on most days, she would stay in bed while I got on with the housework, so she would pay me her £3 too. After school, I would help my mum with two cleaning jobs, which paid me £7 each. At a young age, I had learnt how to earn money!

At the age of fifteen, I went to work in a perfume factory, pretending I was sixteen. Within a couple of weeks, they found out my age and told me to I leave, but because I was a good worker, they said I could return when I was old enough. Within a year of returning there to work, I was made redundant from the factory. Being unemployed and having no money motivated me to job hunt. On the Monday morning, I jumped out of bed bright and early and told myself that I was going out to find a job, and I would not return home until I found one! I knocked on every factory door that day. Almost every factory I approached had no vacancies, but when I got to the very last row, 'Lady Luck shone' (as my Dad would say). I walked into an electrics company. There was no one at reception, so I rang the bell and waited, but there was no reply. As I turned around and walked out the door and back up the path to leave, a rather large gentleman with a bald head and smiley red face started calling to me.

'Excuse me, can I help you?' he called out.

'I'm looking for a job,' I replied.

'Fifty pounds a week in our canteen. Will that do you?'

'Perfect,' I replied.

I skipped and punched the air all the way home. The only reason I got that job was because I was out looking and asking, and this lesson has stayed with me always.

- What do you remember about your 1st wage?

Personal Impact

How did these powerful childhood experiences with money and life affect my behaviour as an adult? To sum it all up, I'd grown up knowing how to earn money, but I never learnt how to manage it properly. Life was also very unsettled, with a lot of emotional turmoil after my parent's divorce. In my early adulthood, I adopted a rebellious attitude like my father. I would work hard and spend hard on clothes and going out socializing. I would often run out of money before payday and sub money from my mum. However, in later years, when debt became my reality, I yearned to be more careful like my mother. And as far as my brothers were concerned, being tight or stealing from people never did appeal to me, so these were good lessons learnt. To this day, my brother William says, *'the likes of you and I weren't meant to have money'*, as he believes that people with money are born into it. I tell him I that chose to believe differently.

Life's lessons are to learn from, not to pass on.

- How do you think your childhood memories affect you as an adult?
- How will any negative money memories affect you if you chose to hold on to them?
- How will your life change if you chose to let them go?

11

Conscious Shopping

Learning to shop consciously will help you to instinctively determine what a good buy is and what isn't. It will enable you to save money because you'll spend a lot less on unwanted items (or trash) that you have got into a regular habit of buying.

CASH = Conscious Action Starts Here

Remember Lisa from the chapter on RED Dot Shopping who said *'for the past twelve years, at least one-third of the items that I have been putting in the trolley have been trash'* This is a fine example of unconscious shopping, since her wakeup call she now shops with her eyes open wide.

Learning to listen to your intuition can enable you to go shopping, enjoy the experience and keep you're spending safe. When this begins to happen, you will become the rightful owner of your wallet and purse; you will be the controller of the shopping trolley. So if you truly do want to make a difference in the way you spend your money and time, then conscious effort is a key ingredient to add.

Spending Intentions

Conscious shopping is designed to get from the start to the finish of your day and keep your spending intact.

- How much money do you intend to spend today?
- How much money do you intend to save?

Ask yourself these questions every morning before leaving home. Write the amount on a Post-it Note and stick it on the fridge, seeing if this marries up when arriving home! As time goes by, this one simple act will become a prevention method to lighten the load of arriving home with too many bags and wondering where all your money has gone. Not only will you save yourself an absolute fortune, but you will waste a lot less of your precious time too. Then you can begin to spend your spare money and time in ways that you want to. Instead of draining your wallet and purse day in and day out, you will fatten it instead.

Habit

Remember that habits have to be learnt, so keep consciously practicing until this simple wealthy spending habit becomes automatic. Acknowledging what your instincts are telling you and listening and adhering to it takes courage and discipline, but when you do, the rewards will far outweigh the choice to ignore what your instincts are telling you. I am sure you don't need reminding of what ignoring them has cost you so far! However, if you do find it hard to keep your spending on track, then keep practicing to RED Dot Shopping. When you are tempted to spend, ask yourself:

- Is it just because I am feeling tired, down, or needy?

And in vulnerable moments such as these, have the courage go home, or back to your car and sit with your feelings. By honouring and acknowledging them, know they will pass. Try sitting quietly and visualising a cloud passing overhead, and with every out breath, it gets further and further away. Gradually the sun gets brighter and you become replenished in a wealthier way and less costly way.

Body Shopping

Or if you are in the shop and feel yourself giving in, stand still, put your hand on your abdomen, and listen to your body's response to sense what your gut feeling is telling you. Call it body shopping! When you do this, you will begin to sense what is right for you and what isn't. You will soon discover that what you think you want materially is not what you inner self is looking for to be fulfilled, as the material possessions are just things that represent feelings. The real you is what truly wants to be expressed, in assertive, confident, and more creative ways than simply buying another bag or dress that resembles yet another plaster. Consciousness shopping will naturally keep your spending habits and behaviours on track and will help you polish up your act. If you stop and ask yourself right now whether you want a life of debt or financial freedom and abundance, which one do you think your consciousness would truly want and chose? Which one excites you the most?

The decision is yours; make it a conscious one.

For Richer

- How much better off would you consciously like to be this time next year?

Just red-dot shopping alone would result in the following:

- If you spent £10 a week less, that would be £520 per year
- If you spent £10 less a day that would be £ 3,650.00 a year!
- Or over 3 years that would be over £10, 950!!

- How much can you 'behave & save' each week?
- Do you get the idea?
- Is the penny dropping?

This can be done so easily by consciously thinking more whilst out shopping as well as during the daily ritual of getting to and from home work, taking the kids to school, or even when take the dog out for a walk, to name a few. Wherever we go or whatever we do, on the journey there and back, we have adopted the habit of popping into the shop, whether we do this consciously or not!

So to sum it up, you'll end up with less trash and more cash. You'll feel empowered as you build your *no* muscle and learn to walk when conscious shopping serves you right.

More *than* Material

It's not the new car that will drive you through life—*no*, only you can do that.
It's not the boob job that will give your image and confidence a boost;
No, that comes from the inside out.
If you wore the same outfit to the Christmas party that you wore last year;
I wonder if your best friend or colleague would comment,
And quite frankly, if they did, the term sad bitch comes to mind!
I put money on it that none of them would.
Go on. I dare you to wear the same outfit as last year and see if anyone says anything.
Being image conscious is all about external images.
The people who are truly worth getting to know,
Are the ones who can see deeper, behind the façade?
And you'd be amazed at how many real and genuine people there are to get to know.
And as for the people who are so wrapped up in how they look;
They definitely aren't interested in you or anyone else;
Unless it's for their own ego or gain.

Icons

Mother Theresa, Jesus, Ghandi, and Florence Nightingale all had the same dress code and outshone all the rest.

Don't Fret

Don't look back and fret about the money have wasted up to now. Instead, just make a conscious decision to get a grip. You cannot change the past, but you can learn from it and move on and make a conscious decision to become better and better in the process.

Learn to disconnect (or unplug) with wasting anymore of your money and time. It's precisely this behaviour that gets you in a money mess. Some days you may be able to think clearly and feel level-headed and connected, acting sensibly. Other days you may feel like hitting the spending switch, especially if your hormones are playing up or if you've generally had a bad day.

- So what can you do to safeguard against sabotaging your wealth?

Perhaps stay at home that day, or only take cash out, or write a list. If you do recognise that you are in a destructive spending mood, know that recognising it in itself is great progress. Also know that the very minute the temptation to spend has an hypnotic affect is when it's at its most powerful, and do whatever you can to snap yourself out of it. Imagine you are disconnecting a plug from a power socket. Then plug your energy in somewhere more fulfilling. Know that the precise moment temptations strikes is when you need to pull back or stand to stare it in the face and smile, knowing you're the one in control! Your body language is a powerful tool to resist, so make a stand. Then, no matter what emotional state you are in, you keep control and win.

Faulty Connection

When you are disconnected, you're clearly not thinking straight. You're shopping in body but not in mind. The following feelings of disharmony can be costly:

- Shopping while tired, hungry, or in a rush
- Shopping in a dazed or hypnotic state
- Feeling stressed and overwhelmed
- Being distracted and easily tempted by offers and bargains

- How do you connect to a good state, in order to be debt-free and have more money and future happiness?

The following exercise will help you. Record this and play it back or get someone to read it to you.

Coming to Your Senses

Close your eyes and imagine arriving at the checkout with just the items that you went in for. As a result, you have money left, and it feels great. As the weeks and months go by, you carry on behaving and saving on each and every shop, and your smart spending habits improve big time. Cher Ching

Money in Imagination

Exercising your imagination gives you the ability to make your dreams reality. You see yourself as you want your situation to be in the future, *not* as it is right now. When you use your imagination, you see yourself through your own eyes. Although you are physically in this moment, you are focusing forwards, and therefore you are associating at a different moment in time than you are presently in.

Imagine yourself feeling confident, managing money well, increasing the amount of money you have, and polishing up your act. Connect with how this makes you feel. When you connect with a good state, you'll begin to feel it and experience it as if it were real. This is because your mind doesn't distinguish true from false or now from future. It simply accepts what you tell it and responds accordingly. And as you set the scene, or sow the seed in your mind, it then sets to work nurturing and growing the seed you have planted. Subconsciously, your mind begins the search, and I guarantee it won't be long before you attract like with like, because that's the law of creation. But first you have to imagine and create it in your mind, just as if you were a child again playing an imaginary game, allowing your thoughts to get carried away. Whether you believe this or think it's a load of tosh, just try it. What do you have to lose?

When you choose to disbelieve, you won't get good results. You will get results, but only on the level you are vibrating out, and hence you'll attract like with like. You have heard the saying that *'we get what we ask for'*, and it's so true.

Well Connected

When you are well connected, you are confident and in control of spending money. You have the qualities described below:

3. Calm and relaxed—in control of your trolley
4. Totally focused—not distracted in the slightest
5. Enjoying the experience—feeling calmly content
6. Intuitive—instincts serving you well
7. In the flow—tuned into decent offers and opportunities that will be definite money savers

Reconnect

Learn to reconnect your mindset to images, pictures, words, and feelings that connect you—a feeling of being excellent with money, rich beyond measure, happy from the inside out, or whatever it is you want to imagine. Imagine that you are plugging your thinking into a more powerful socket.

Begin to have conversations with your money and ask it what it thinks (crazy, I know, but give it a go!). Ask your money, 'If I decide to spend you, will the item I'm buying be an asset or a liability?' When you receive money, say thank you and give it the respect and value it is worth. Then watch as it pays you back! One rich guy kisses his money each time he receives it. Someone recently stated that if all the money in the world were equally divided, it would soon return to the people who looked after it the most! Wouldn't you?

The Paradox of Our Age

We have bigger houses but smaller families,
More conveniences, but less time;
We have more degrees, but less sense;
More knowledge, but less judgment;
More experts, but more problems;
More medicines, but less healthiness;

Hey Big Spender 'get an emotional grip'

We've been all the way to the moon and back;
But have trouble crossing the street to meet the new neighbour.
We built more computers to hold more information to produce
more copies than ever,
But less communication;
We have become long on quantity, but short on quality.
These are the times of fast foods, but slow digestion;
Tall men but short character;
Steep profits but shallow relationships;
It's the time when there is much in the window,
but nothing in the room

                                                    The Dalai Lama

12

Budge *it*

For an emotional spender, learning to budget is a challenge at first, as your buying decisions have been made by the heart, not the head. Even after following the budgeting process, there's no guarantee that you will pay attention to it the next time the urge to mend and spend kicks in. But budgeting is a significant part of adopting better spending habits and planning ahead. Plus, the tasks in life that meet the most resistance are often the ones that you need to do and will benefit greatly from. At first, budgeting may seem a boring or complicated task, especially if you've never prepared one. Plus the use of debit cards, credit cards, direct debits, as well as receiving money electronically means you have lots of bank statements and paperwork to sort through. But don't use this as the perfect excuse to not start!

- **So why should I bother?** A budget enables you to do the following:

- Look at ways to increase your income and build wealth
- Set healthy financial boundaries and build your NO muscle
- Know exactly where you stand and get back in control
- Recognise and plug your money leaks

If you don't know where you stand with your money, then someone else will easily take control of your financial destiny, especially when your money runs out. It's so easy to buy products and services on credit and not knowing if your money will stretch, not to mention the added interest it will cost you. I know a big part of your RED behaviour would prefer not to even go there. However it should be in your utmost interest to stop and take a look at the budget and then make the buying decision, not the other way round!

Stretch your mind stretch your money

Get Creative

Don't start by thinking of complicated figures. Instead see your budget as a container of water *or* liquid gold; your aim is to see the money levels filling up and up, until they one day overflow. Each time you emotionally spend beyond your budget, know that your money and happiness drain with it. However, for every spending leak you plug and every tempting offer that you turn down, you will be the one growing richer not the retailer, now doesn't that put a smile on your face? Whose container would you prefer to fill? If your budget were a container, what would the money inside it look like?

- Full and overflowing with plenty in reserve
- Draining out a lot faster than it comes in
- Very low on resources
- Totally empty running on fumes
- Which one would you like it to be?

The aim is to get more money flowing in than out so you can sleep at night and build wealth. The budgeting process doesn't appear to be exciting or fun at first, but it's an absolute must if you want to keep track of your money. It's also a way of communicating and planning what you want from your money as an individual or together as a family.

Why do some people bother and others don't?

One in three adults refuses to plan money. They either don't know where to start or are too afraid to look. Birthdays, weddings, holidays, and even funerals are planned, but when it comes to planning money, it is way down the list of priorities.

A remedy for conquering any budgeting fear is to try it 3 times in the first month:

1. Once to practice and get over any fears
2. Second to find out how to do it in more detail.
3. Thirdly to get better and better at it

After that it's a piece of cake. Put a date in the diary and plan the first 3 times and once a month thereafter. If this includes you and the family make sure they can be there.

Personally, I didn't budget for over thirty years. No wonder this act of neglect and little respect for my money led to massive debt. Firstly, I never knew how to prepare a budget. Secondly, it seemed a daunting process that I thought was for accountants and intelligent people. Thirdly, I never knew the true value of the process. I roughly knew how much money was coming in and going out, so I assumed that was all I needed to know. And when I did have an incline that more money was going out than I could afford I simply ignored it. But looking back, if I'd learnt this process and put it into practice a lot earlier on in my life, then it may have prevented my careless spending habits from spiralling so out of control. It was only when I financially hit rock bottom that I began to learn the budgeting art.

Preparing Your Budget

Your budget's a record or reading of your money. The budgeting process takes time and patience at the start. If you get overwhelmed with it, either set yourself a goal to revisit the task

Ann Carver

until you've completed it or ask for help from a family member or friend or a reputable organization such as Citizen Advice Bureau.

Decide who it's for

Before you start a budget, you'll need to decide if it is just for you or if it also includes your spouse/partner/family. It's better if everyone concerned joins in and learns the budgeting process together. This is important if decisions have to be made about changes in what everyone spends. And to teach the kids at an early age is the best thing you could do.

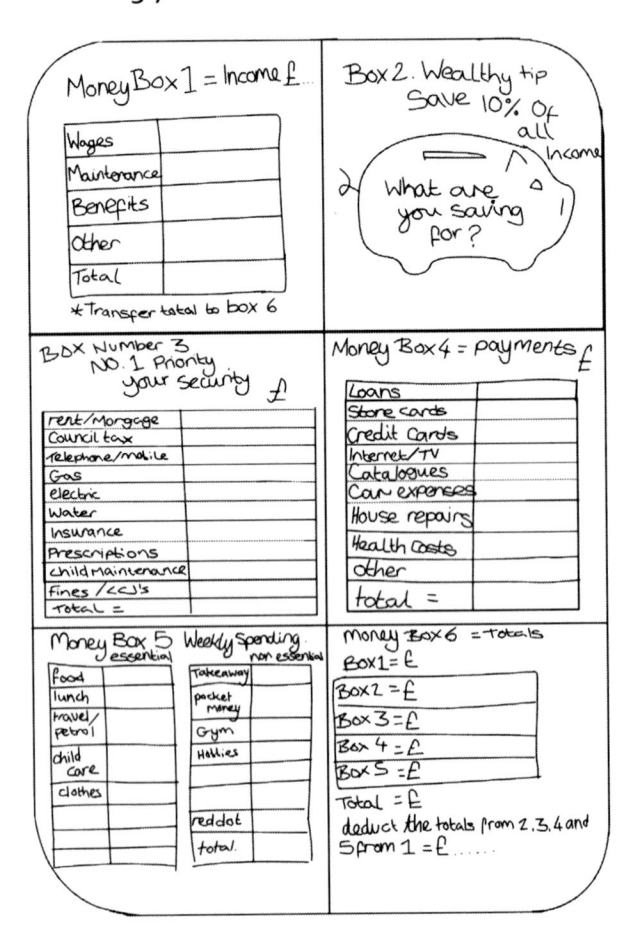

Money Box 1 = Income £		Box 2. Wealthy tip Save 10% of all income
Wages		What are you saving for?
Maintenance		
Benefits		
Other		
Total		
*Transfer total to box 6		

Box Number 3 — No. 1 Priority your security £		Money Box 4 = payments £
rent/mortgage		Loans
Council tax		Store cards
Telephone/mobile		Credit Cards
Gas		Internet/TV
electric		Catalogues
Water		Car expenses
Insurance		House repairs
Prescriptions		Health costs
child maintenance		other
Fines/CCJ's		total =
Total =		

Money Box 5 Weekly Spending			
essential		non essential	
Food		Takeaway	
lunch		pocket money	
travel/petrol		Gym	
child care		Hobbies	
clothes			
		red dot	
		total	

Money Box 6 = Totals
Box 1 = £
Box 2 = £
Box 3 = £
Box 4 = £
Box 5 = £
Total = £
deduct the totals from 2,3,4 and 5 from 1 = £......

Hey Big Spender 'get an emotional grip'

The Budge *it* Sheet

This has 3 aspects 1) Earn 2) Save 3)Spend

Money Box 1 = Earn Record *all* the money that comes into your household

Money Box 2 = Save 10% of all money as soon as hits your bank account. Set up a savings account with the highest interest rate you can get (research online). Ask your bank to transfer 10% electronically by direct debit. If any extra money comes in take out 10% and save that too. Have a 10% savings pot in your home. Make sure the kids have one as well.

To calculate 10% = If your income is £2,570, divide by 10 = £257. Transfer figure to budget sheet. Decide what you want to save for. I want to save for..

Remember out of £100, you get to keep £90 and save £10

Money Box 3 = Spend on your security; this means pay all the bills listed in box 3, as these keep the roof over your head and the wolves from the door. Have a good look at your bank statements and find out exactly what you are paying and to whom. If any of the costs seem too high, give the company a call and maybe look to change supplier.

Money Box 4 = Spend on creditors. Find out exactly what you are paying and to whom. See how much any credit cards, loans, and so forth are costing you in interest. Shop around for better deals. If you are overwhelmed and cannot afford to pay, call the Consumer Credit Counselling Services 0800 138 1111

Box 5 = Weekly Spending for food shopping, travel and kid's money etc. Calculate how much you need for each, also include the total you are impulse spending from week to week (refer to RED Dot Shopping). Know that Money Box 3 & 4 should be priority over emotional and impulse spending! If you're paid monthly, make sure enough money is put aside to cover all your weekly costs. If it helps divide it into 4 pots. Make sure you avoid going overdrawn to stop incurring charges, or open a basic bank account where you can't go overdrawn.

Box 6 = Total Transfer the totals from each Money Box into Box 6. Deduct Boxes 2,3,4 & 5 from Box 1. Do you have money left over or not enough to go round? Once again if there is more money going out than in call 0800 138 1111 and ask for help.

Money Leaks

In the box below, list the items that are causing your budget to leak the most. Also refer to RED Dot shopping.

How can you stop the leaks and increase your income?

One small leak can sink an entire ship.
—Benjamin Franklin

Balance

Unfortunately, money has been used and abused by people from all walks of life. When human greed takes hold, people will beg, borrow, or steal to have their fill of it. And to be frank, there's absolutely nothing you or I can do about others but learn to love and respect money and life for ourselves. Regardless of whether you have a little or a lot, it's definitely what you decide to do with it that counts.

13

Real Stories Real People

Jeff

Jeff telephoned me confessing to be a recovered spendaholic who, like me, wanted to help others. As I listened to Jeff's story, I admired his honesty, although I sensed that part of him was holding back, just as I had. I asked Jeff what caused his debt. Jeff had run up over £100,000 in credit card debt before his wife found out the true extent. He said to me that his problem was pure greed, but something inside me thought that there was more to it than that. However, I didn't push for answers at such an early stage of conversation. I knew that his debt and the self-blame attitude were humble of him, but that he was also disguising the root of the problem, as I had. Our similarities and mannerisms made it evident that we had a lot in common. Jeff had contacted me a few weeks before our meeting, as he had heard about the work I was doing, so we arranged to meet. The first hour of our conversation was surface stuff, talking about debt and the lack of available help to assist with the underlying causes. Jeff and his wife, Jean, were looking to set up a signpost organization that would enable people in debt to know where to get the right type of help. I thought his idea was good, although I said to Jeff that he looked more than a signpost to me. He laughed, but at the same time, I knew that he could be an icon for so many others, if only I could convince him to wear his heart on his sleeve and to nurture being authentic.

I then shared my story with them. I firmly believe that in order to embark on a journey of true debt freedom, we must leave *no stone unturned*. I knew I owed it to myself and the people I met along the way to find and uproot the problem.

My personal debt was deep rooted like Jeff's. And like Jeff, I had chosen to bury mine deep down in my soul, where I thought it would stay; however, all this did was enable my problems to grow like bloody mushrooms in the dark. But as I was on my journey of recovery, I knew I had to get to the root of it all, for I wanted to be debt-free, truly debt-free. Paying my debts back was literally the first step on the journey to reversing the adversity that had affected me for most of my life. The second and most significant step was paying the debt back that I owed to myself, and that was to learn to love Ann for who she is, to accept her just as she is. This step for me was a very gradual process.

All in good time

When the moment's right, your healing process will be revealed to you as it was to me. I know this is why my personal revelation naturally unfolded over a number of years. As I look back, I can recall a number of significant experiences. One moment was when I was camping in Devon. On the first night, I awoke desperately needing the loo, but at the same time, I was scared to go out in the dark. Reluctantly, I ventured out into the night, to my surprise I was met with a magnificent blanket of stars, they were a lot brighter from the polluted city where I lived. Then a shooting star made fast tracks across the sky, and I stood in awesome wonder, thinking, *if I can be brave enough to a stand tall in the dark of it all, I will see the stars.*

Going back to the night I met Jeff, it was the first time on this journey that I met almost a carbon copy of me. I have met lots of people with spending problems, and many great people who have believed and supported the cause, but never anyone who could mirror me in so many ways. I shared my story with Jeff and Jean, and then Jeff shared his story too. He said he could relate to my story.

When Jeff was a child, he was sexually molested, and although his parents knew, this was hidden. He was also beaten by his father apart from Christmas, where his father would pull out all the stops to make this event a happy time. In later years, as a husband and father, Jeff would make Christmas a massive event and spend a lot of money, as he had a deep emotional connection to this, plus like me, he shopped to hide the guilt and shame he had carried around since he was a child. I felt truly honoured when Jeff shared the truth about the root of his spending problem. I also know the importance of doing this, for this is where true healing begins, as the light of day can pour into the hidden depths and heal our wounds. Jeff's debt was not about his personal greed at all. It was much deeper rooted than that. And like me, he is now emotionally free of it all and using his journey to help others.

Bridgette

Bridgette is sharing her story as part of her healing process, this was a big and courageous thing for her to do, *thank you Bridgette.*

I became a single mum at the age of thirty-one; my two children were eighteen months and three years old. I was on benefits until I was thirty-six, and I managed to live on a very small budget. When I started work full time again I was debt-free.

I received offers from loan companies to apply for credit cards (this hadn't happened to me before I'd started work). I was seduced almost immediately and began to treat myself and my children to all the things I felt we had missed out on over the past few years. I felt happy, and it was so nice to be able to go on holiday and have days out. I loved the emotional high I got from buying things. I used up the entire credit card and then got a new one with 0% interest and transferred the debt. And so the cycle began, using the credit and then transferring it, until I had too many cards, and my access to obtaining credit stopped.

That was when reality kicked in. I tried my best to keep up with the minimum payments, but despite best efforts, I failed. This meant I either paid late or missed payments, and the debt grew and grew. It was a gradual process that took a total of fifteen years, but eventually, when I was brave enough to face it, the debt totalled £25,000.

My health suffered, and I developed asthma and irritable bowel syndrome. I kept thinking, all will be OK. I will win the lottery, or someone will give me the money. Anything except facing the truth . . . It was at this point that I confided in my sister and admitted the reality of my situation. She rang me a few days later and said she had spoken to her husband; they had both decided to lend me the money to clear my debt. An arrangement was made that I would pay back the money within three years.

To be honest, at that point, from a selfish point of view, I didn't really think how I was going to repay it. I just thought, I want the phone calls and the post to stop. My debt was something I thought about 24/7. It was like a dark cloud hanging over me, and I was thoroughly miserable. It consumed my every waking moment.

My sister and brother-in-law lent me the money to pay all the debt; however, it wasn't, as all I'd done was move it somewhere else. Over the next year, my relationship with my brother-in-law deteriorated to the point that we had a huge argument and he told me never to go to his house again. This caused a family rift and resulted in my being isolated from some members of my family.

I was then made redundant, and this impacted my debt further, as I borrowed £8,000 from other members of my family. It sounds awful now, but I genuinely could not see how bad things were. I was just hoping for a miracle. A meeting was called at my dad's house, with everyone present, and my family sat around and discussed my predicament and how I was to raise the funds to repay the money. They sat round me as if I were on trial, and I can honestly say that I had never felt so ashamed of myself. It was truly the lowest point in my life. I felt wretched. I went home, and after I stopped feeling sorry for myself, I realised that I had to do something about this to regain my self-esteem and pride and take control of the money before it consumed me forever.

I have a good friend with a lovely husband, and I valued his opinion greatly. He would always tell me the truth, whether I wanted to hear it or not. He advised me to sell my house (I had lived there for twenty-three years. At this point, my children were now twenty and twenty-two years old.) I decided that this was my only chance, so I rang the estate agent in the morning and put my home on the market. I sold the house and had to move out within eight weeks! It was a huge wrench, and the day I moved was brutal, but I knew I had done the right thing.

So many people advised me to go bankrupt, move abroad, and so forth, but I felt that it was my debt. I had gotten my family and myself into this mess, and I had to be the one to get us out. Within three weeks of moving, I had paid all the money back to my family, every penny.

I cannot begin to tell you how happy I am now. I live in rented accommodations and work full time again. Both my children have been to university and got degrees, and everything I own now is paid for. I had to sell my house, but I wouldn't go back to that for anything, as I am debt free. I only buy things I want if I have the money. I do not have credit cards, loans, or owe anybody anything. I feel so proud of myself that I finally came to my senses and regained my power and control over my life.

Money needs to work for you; it shouldn't be the other way round. I would never go back to that way of living, but it was so easy to get myself into it. I now have a different view of money, and I have saved a little. It is a start, and I have learned to respect money. I know it's a cliché, but if I can do it, you can too!

Don't be scared as you can turn your life around in the process. It takes brave decisions and heartache sometimes, but it is so worth it, believe me. Good luck.

Sarah's Story

From having a well paid job and no money worries, to experiencing financial loss, downsizing the home and renting and having a part time self employed job, it has been very difficult for me to adjust to my current circumstances. I.e. budgeting and saving. Then I heard about the Hey Big Spender course and decided to go along. My goal was to learn how to manage my money better and save. Having a small income, more goes out than comes in, which needed addressing. I also don't want to be dependent on my husband bailing me out. As a result I am saving 10% of my money the moment in comes in and I also realised that I am still 'grieving' the life I used to have.

I am learning to appreciate and value what I have now and there are a, lot of benefits-I have a fantastic relationship with my husband, which has grown stronger since our financial glitch, I have good friends, I am keeping busy being self employed and now I feel I can save and use it to invest in future goals. It has helped me to realise I can mange my money. I have also seen where I have been going wrong with red dot shopping. And the emotional baggage that I have been carrying around about money has also come to light and am moving on from that. I am now cultivating a better relationship with money.

The Stairway

Emotional freedom equals no guilt, no shame, no hiding, no bitterness, no looking over your shoulder, and no hate. One thing is for sure: debt bought me to my knees. Debt taught me to have faith and believe that one day it'd be all right. It taught me to find my voice as a woman, to speak out in truth, to appreciate the simple things in life, and to value my life and my small but close family. Emotional freedom taught me to love and accept myself just as I am and to detach myself from people who undermined me. I know it's my destiny to help others find debt freedom on all levels, to help them be emotionally, mindfully, and spiritually as one. Reaching out to help others reach up and out of their debt crisis is where the true stairway to heaven lies.

What's your story? Reflecting on what you have read, what have you learnt about you and your relationship with money? Maybe you have your very own book inside of you? I urge you to put a pen to paper and create something beautiful.

A BIG CREDIT to YOU Ann Carver

Help Line References

Many of the contacts listed are head offices. Contact them to obtain the local office in your area and check their websites for more details.

Say NO to 0870

The site lists many well-known companies and their equivalent geographical numbers.

Alternatives listed for 0500, 0800, 0808, 0842, 0843, 0844, 0845, 0870, 0871, 0872, and 0873 numbers.
www.SAYNOTO0870.COM

Action on Addiction
Call 0300 330 0659
www.actiononaddiction.org.uk

Age Concern
(Advice about money, benefits, and other issues)
0800 00 99 66
www.ageconcern.co.uk

Business Debtline
(Debt advice for self-employed and small business)
0800 197 6026
www.bdl.org.uk

Citizen Advice Bureaux
(Offering independent advice on a range of issues)
www.citizensadvice.org.uk

Community Legal Advice
(Agencies offering legal advice)
0845 345 4345
www.communitylegaladvice.org.uk

Consumer Credit Counselling Services
(Free advice on problem debt based on what's best for you)
0800 138 1111
www.cccs.co.uk

Consumer Direct
(Helpline for consumer and fuel problems)
0845 404 0506
www.consumerdirect.gov.uk

Cruse
(Advice and support for people dealing with death)
0844 477 9400
www.crusebereavementcare.org.uk

Drinkline
(Provides help if you are worried about your alcohol habits)
0800 731 4314
www.drinksmarter.org.uk

Financial Ombudsman Service
(For complaints about banks, building societies, loans and credit, hire purchase, mortgages, insurance, investments, endowment polices, and pensions)
0845 080 1800
www.financial-ombudsman.org.uk

Gamblers Anonymous
(Provides help on how to deal with gambling problems)
020 7384 3040
www.gamblersanonymous.org.uk

Life Centre
(Support survivors of rape and sexual abuse and their supporters)
0844 847 7879
www.lifecentre.uk.com

Hey Big Spender 'get an emotional grip'

Money Advice Trust
(Reputable UK money advice)
0808 808 4000
www.nationaldebtline.co.uk

Mind
(A charity and helpline which helps with mental health problems)
0845 7660 163
www.mind.org.uk

National Domestic Violence Helpline
(Support and information for people experiencing domestic violence)
0808 200 0247
www.refuge.org.uk

National Drugs Helpline
(Information and advice about drugs)
0800 77 66 00
www.talktofrank.com

Payplan
(Provides free debt management service)
0800 085 4298
www.payplan.com

Relate
(Advice and counselling to help with relationship problems)
0300 100 1234
www.relate.org.uk

Rights for Women
(Legal advice for women)
020 7251 6577
www.rightsforwomen.org.uk

Ann Carver

Samaritans
(Confidential emotional support)
0845 790 9090
www.samaritans.org

Shelter
(Free housing advice helpline)
0808 800 4444
www.shelter.org.uk

Stop Loan Sharks
(Confidentially report a loan shark)
0300 555 2222
www.stoploansharks.direct.gov.uk

TaxAid
(Advice about tax problems)
0845 120 3779
www.taxaid.org.uk

Triumph Over Phobia (TOP UK)
(Helps sufferers of phobias, obsessive compulsive disorder, and other related anxiety to overcome their fears and become ex-sufferers)
0845 600 9601
www.topuk.org.uk

EDUCATION

Fielding Financial Family
(Educating and empowering families to establish their own wealth)
01926 629028
www.fieldingfinancialfamily.com

Hey Big Spender
(Enabling people to recognise and address emotional and impulsive spending habits)
www.heybigspenders.co.uk

The Coaching Academy
(Coaching courses offer an unrivalled quality of training for coaches. Train as a personal coach, corporate coach, small business coach, NLP practitioner, or a youth coach)
0208 4399 440
www.the-coaching-academy.com

School for Social Entrepreneurs
(Provides learning and support to social entrepreneurs in UK and around the world)
www.sse.org.uk

Tony Robbins
Tony Robbins has developed a series of books, tapes, seminars, multimedia packages, and coaching systems that are utilised by people worldwide in the improvement of their physical health, emotional well-being, relationships, finances, time management, and professional growth.
www.anthony-robbins.org.uk

Transforming Debt to Wealth Programme
With John Cummuta
(Information products and free downloads)
www.johncummuta.com

Ann Carver

Stopping Overshopping with April Benson (USA)
www.Shopaholicnomore.com

Recommended Reading

Riches, by Gill Fielding
7 secrets of wealth the common man was never told

Sheconomics, by Karen Pine and Simonne Gnesson
Add power to your purse with the ultimate money makeover

Smart Women Finish Rich, by David Bach
Step-by-step plan for achieving financial security and funding your dreams

The Riches Within, by Dr. John F. Martini
Learn how to empower yourself and live authentically

Think and Grow Rich, by Napoleon Hill
Worldwide bestseller on mindset and money

The Millionaire Messenger, by Brendon Berchard
Share your life story and make a difference

To Buy or Not to Buy, by April Benson
Why we overshop and how to stop
You Can Get It If You Really Want, by Levi Roots
Start your business and transform your life